KALLIS' iBT TOEFL® PATTERN

Speaking 2

KALLIS' iBT TOEFL® Pattern Speaking 2

KALLIS EDU, INC.
7490 Opportunity Road, Suite 203
San Diego, CA 92111
(858) 277-8600
info@kallisedu.com
www.kallisedu.com

ISBN-10: 1-5004-4395-6
ISBN-13: 978-1-5004-4395-5

iBT TOEFL® Pattern - Speaking II is the second of our three-level iBT TOEFL® Speaking Exam preparation book series.

Our **iBT TOEFL® Pattern Speaking** series simplifies each TOEFL speaking task into a series of simple steps, which ensures that students do not become overwhelmed as they develop their speaking skills. Moreover, our commitment to minimizing instruction and maximizing student practice assures that students have many opportunities to strengthen their speaking skills.

KALLIS

KALLIS'

TOEFL® iBT PATTERN

SPEAKING 2

CONFIDENCE

Getting Started

A study guide should familiarize the reader with the material found on the test, develop unique methods that can be used to solve various question types, and provide practice questions to challenge future test-takers. *KALLIS' iBT TOEFL® Pattern Series* aims to accomplish all these study tasks by presenting iBT TOEFL® test material in an organized, comprehensive, and easy-to-understand way.

KALLIS' iBT TOEFL® Pattern Speaking Series provides in-depth explanations and practices that will help you prepare for the iBT TOEFL speaking section. This study guide focuses on the development of simple, step-by-step response strategies that will guide you when responding to each speaking task.

Understanding the Speaking Tasks

Chapters 1 through 6 are devoted to explaining and solving each of the six speaking tasks. The beginning of each of these chapters introduces one of the six types of speaking tasks encountered in the iBT TOEFL speaking section. These introductory sections will prepare you for the explanations and practices that follow.

General Information

The **General Information** section presents the speaking skills that you will need to complete the speaking portion of the iBT TOEFL and provides descriptions of each speaking task.

Hacking Strategy

The **Hacking Strategy** and corresponding **Example** provide a step-by-step process that explains how to prepare for and respond to each speaking task. While the **Hacking Strategy** develops a common process that can be used to respond to any speaking task, the **Example** demonstrates how this common process can be used to solve one particular type of speaking task.

Improving Speaking Skills through Practice

A combination of explanations and practices breaks down each speaking task into simple, step-by-step processes.

Practices

In Chapters 1 through 6, each step of the **Hacking Strategy** is elaborated on with a brief explanation and with one or more **Practices**. These provide opportunities to develop the skills that you just read about. Each **Practice** builds upon information presented earlier in the chapter, allowing you to gradually develop skills that you will use when you are responding to the speaking tasks.

Exercises

Exercises require you to use skills developed in each chapter to complete a speaking task response. Each **Exercise** provides a series of templates that help you organize and compose your response; after each **Exercise**, you will find an Evaluation page that allows you to check the effectiveness of your response. Three **Exercises** are located at the end of each of the task-specific chapters (Chapters 1 through 6).

Actual Practice

Chapter 7 consists of three/five **Actual Practices**, which provide templates to help you outline and compose Independent and Integrated speaking responses. Thus, **Actual Practices** require you to use skills from all **Practices**, so **Actual Practices** should only be attempted after you are familiar with the structure of the iBT TOEFL speaking section.

Actual Test

The **Actual Test** section, which is located in Chapter 8, presents all six speaking tasks in a format that resembles the official iBT TOEFL writing test. Because this section does not contain the detailed templates given in the **Exercises** or the **Actual Practices**, this section should be attempted only after all speaking skills have been mastered.

In Case You Need Help

- ▶ Toward the back of this book, you will find the **Answer Key**, which provides model answers to the **Practices** from Chapters 1 through 6. Additionally, model answers are included immediately after their corresponding **Exercises** and **Actual Practices/Test**.
- ▶ These model answers demonstrate one acceptable way to answer each question, but there will often be many acceptable answers. So do not feel that your responses must be the same as the model answers, just use them for guidance when necessary.

Table of Contents

INDEPENDENT SPEAKING

Chapter 1

Chapter 2

INTEGRATED SPEAKING

Chapter 3

Chapter 4

Ready, Set, Speak!

Before You Begin...

INDEPENDENT AND INTEGRATED TASKS

The iBT TOEFL Speaking test consists of six tasks: two Independent tasks and four Integrated tasks.

The first two tasks are called "Independent tasks" because they require you to produce a response without using any extra written or spoken materials. Thus, you must come up with responses to the first two tasks independently, using your own experiences or opinions.

The last four tasks are called "Integrated tasks" because they require you to incorporate, or integrate, material from spoken and/or written sources into your response. Task 3, for example, will require you to read a passage, listen to a conversation, and then form a response based on what you have read and heard. Two of the Integrated tasks deal with university-related issue, and the other two Integrated tasks discuss academic topics that reflect material that an American-university student might encounter.

TRANSITION WORDS AND PHRASES

Transition words and phrases explain how the content of one sentence relates to the rest of your response.

Meaning	Examples
addition	*additionally, furthermore, in addition, in fact, moreover*
cause-and-effect	*as a result, consequently, then, therefore, to this end*
compare/contrast	*compared to, despite, however, in contrast, on the contrary, on the one hand, on the other hand, nevertheless*
conclusions	*finally, in conclusion, in summary, lastly, thus, in short*
examples	*for example, for instance, in this case, in this situation*
introductions	*according to, as indicated in/by, based on*
reasons	*one reason is, another reason is, due to*
sequence	*afterward, again, also, and, finally, first, next, previously, second, third*

SYMBOLS AND ABBREVIATIONS

When taking notes to prepare for a spoken response, save time by using symbols and abbreviations instead of complete words. You can create your own symbols and abbreviations in addition to using those listed in the charts on the following page.

Symbol	Meaning	Symbol	Meaning
&	and	=	equals, is
%	percent	>	more than
#	number	<	less than
@	at	→	resulting in
↓	decreasing	↑	increasing

ABBREVIATIONS FOR UNIVERSITY ACTIVITIES

Abbreviation	Meaning	Abbreviation	Meaning
edu.	education	RA	resident assistant
GE	general education	stu.	student
GPA	grade point average	TA	teaching assistant
prof.	professor/professional	univ.	university

ABBREVIATIONS FOR ACADEMIC TOPICS

Abbreviation	Meaning	Abbreviation	Meaning
bio.	biology/biological	exp.	experience/experiment
c.	century	info.	information
chem.	chemistry/chemical	gov.	government
def.	definition	hyp.	hypothesis
econ.	economics/economy	phys.	physics/physical
env.	environment	psych.	psychology/psychological
ex.	example	sci.	science/scientific

OTHER ABBREVIATIONS

Abbreviation	Meaning	Abbreviation	Meaning
abt.	about	pic.	picture
b/c	because	ppl.	people
comm.	community/communication	pref.	preference
e/o	each other	pt.	point
fam.	family	ques.	question
fav.	favorite	s/b	somebody
gen.	general/generation	s/o	someone
hr.	hour	sec.	second
impt.	important	w/	with
loc.	location	w/i	within
lvl.	level	w/o	without
min.	minute	yr.	year

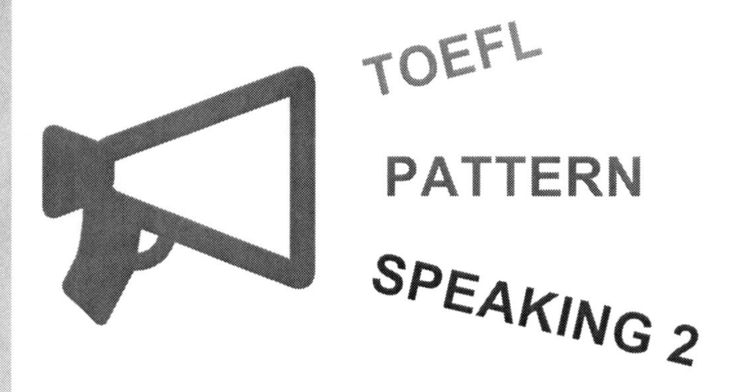

Task 1

CHAPTER 1

Sharing a Personal Experience

Sharing a Personal Experience

GENERAL BACKGROUND INFORMATION

1. EXPLANATION OF TASK 1

You will be asked to speak about a personal experience or familiar topic. A narrator will read the prompt aloud; the prompt will stay on the computer screen during your preparation and response time.

You will then have 15 seconds to prepare your response. Begin preparing when the "Preparation Time" notice appears on your screen. Use the time to write down a few notes in outline form because you will not have enough time to write a full answer.

At the end of 15 seconds, you will hear a short beep. The "Preparation Time" notice changes to "Response Time." The countdown from 45 seconds begins. Your response will be recorded during the 45 seconds. At the end, the recording will stop. A new screen will indicate that the response time has ended.

2. NECESSARY SKILLS FOR TASK 1

You must be able to:

- recall personal experiences and events and form opinions about them
- organize ideas coherently with a clear topic statement and supporting reasons
- speak clearly using correct grammar, vocabulary, and pronunciation

3. EXPLANATION OF QUESTION TYPES

You will see one of two types of questions for the personal experience prompt. In both types of prompt, you must state an opinion and support that opinion with reasons and details.

Question Types

1 Describing a Familiar Person, Place, Activity, or Event

Describe X. Explain how X has affected your life. Use specific reasons and details to support your answer.

2 Expressing Personal Likes, Dislikes, or Values

Describe your favorite/least favorite X. Explain why X is your favorite/least favorite. Use specific reasons and examples to support your answer.

4. EXAMPLE PROMPTS

Possible Task 1 prompts that you may encounter on the official TOEFL exam include:

Prompt

- Describe the most disappointing moment in your life. Explain why this moment was so disappointing. Include details to support your answer.
- What factors do you consider when you choose a restaurant? Use reasons and details to support your answer.
- If you could go anywhere in the world, where would you like to go? Use specific reasons and details to support your answer.
- Describe the most important quality of a good teacher. Explain why this quality is so important. Support your answer with reasons and details.
- What is the most impressive book you have read? Include reasons and details to support your answer.
- What is the best way to stay healthy? Give reasons and examples to support your answer.

5. USEFUL EXPRESSIONS

Some useful expressions for Task 1 are:

- I think (that) ___________.
- I believe (that) ___________.
- In my experience, ___________.
- The most ___________ is ___________ because ___________.
- The best ___________ is ___________ because ___________.
- The worst ___________ is ___________ because ___________.
- My favorite ___________ is ___________ because ___________.
- My least favorite ___________ is ___________ because ___________.

HACKING STRATEGY

STEP 1. OUTLINE YOUR RESPONSE

- Read the prompt carefully
- Decide on an opinion

STEP 2. PREPARE YOUR RESPONSE

- Make your opinion into a topic statement
- Add reasons that support your opinion

STEP 3. DELIVER YOUR RESPONSE

- Respond using coherent sentences
- Add transition words between ideas

STEP 1. Outline Your Response

First, you must read the prompt carefully. Make sure that you understand exactly what the prompt is asking you to do.

Prompt

Describe a time in your life when you had a problem and received help. Who helped you, and how did he or she help? Use specific reasons and details to support your answer.

For this prompt, the first thing that you must do is to select a memory to describe. Your response to the main part of the prompt is called your *opinion*. After reading the prompt, quickly write down your opinion. Make sure that you choose something that you can talk about for 45 seconds.

- Opinion: *programming class too hard → teaching assistant helped*

STEP 2. Prepare Your Response

When organizing your response, you should make your opinion into a topic statement and come up with at least two reasons or details that support your topic statement. Because you are only given 15 seconds to prepare for your response, you must organize your thoughts quickly.

- Topic Statement: *Once I took a computer programming class that was too hard for me, but a teaching assistant gave me so much help that I managed to pass.*
  - Reason 1: *TA believed in me*
  - Reason 2: *TA → patient & very calm*

STEP 3. Deliver Your Response

Use the outline that you created in STEP 2 to guide you as you deliver your response. Respond using complete sentences, and add transition words to show how ideas relate to one another.

Once I took a computer programming class that was too hard for me, but a teaching assistant gave me so much help that I managed to pass. During the first few weeks of the class, I felt overwhelmed, but I attended section meetings with a teaching assistant who helped me in two ways. ***First***, *he seemed confident that I could learn the concepts, which in turn boosted my confidence.* ***Second***, *he was very patient and didn't mind explaining even the most difficult concepts from the class to me.*

STEP 1. OUTLINE YOUR RESPONSE

APPROACHING A PROMPT

Make sure that you respond to the entire prompt. One prompt will often ask you to address multiple points.

Prompt

What is one skill or lesson that you have learned from the Internet rather than from school? Use specific reasons and details to support your answer.

This prompt is instructing you to address related points. You are being asked to

1) describe something you learned from the Internet
2) explain your answer

Additionally, the prompt will always tell you to use *specific* reasons, details, and/or examples.

FORMING AN OPINION

After reading the prompt, you must form an opinion that addresses the prompt. Because you only have 15 seconds to outline your entire response, coming up with an opinion quickly is crucial.

Prompt

What is one skill or lesson that you have learned from the Internet rather than from school? Use specific reasons and details to support your answer.

Make sure that you choose an opinion that is familiar to you and simple enough to explain in 45 seconds. And remember, you are being scored based on how well you defend your opinion, not based on what particular opinion you select.

Because you should decide on your opinion immediately after reading the prompt, use short phrases to state your opinion.

- Opinion: *treat sore throat*

Quickly come up with an opinion, write it on the blank line, and then give a reason that supports your selection.

1) My favorite type of music is *classical music* because *listening to it helps me relax*.

2) My favorite movie is ______________ because ______________________________.

3) My favorite color is ______________ because ______________________________.

4) My favorite author is ______________ because ______________________________.

5) My favorite subject in school is ______________ because ______________________________.

6) My favorite animal is ______________ because ______________________________.

7) My favorite season is ______________ because ______________________________.

8) My favorite city is ______________ because ______________________________.

PRACTICE 2

Write down your opinion for each of the prompts below.

1) **Prompt**

To whom do you usually go when you want advice regarding a problem or a difficult situation?

- Opinion: ______________________________

2) **Prompt**

Describe one of your earliest memories.

- Opinion: ______________________________

3) **Prompt**

What famous person have you frequently admired?

- Opinion: ______________________________

STEP 2A. PREPARE YOUR RESPONSE

FORMING A TOPIC STATEMENT

The **topic statement** should be the first sentence of your speaking response. It gives your opinion in the form of a statement. Make sure that you choose an opinion that you can support with reasons and details for 45 seconds.

Create a topic statement by including vocabulary from the prompt to provide a clear and concise response to the prompt.

Prompt

What is one skill or lesson that you have learned from the Internet rather than from school? Use specific reasons and details to support your answer.

- Opinion: *treat sore throat*

- Topic Statement: *One skill I learned from the Internet was how to treat a sore throat.*

Note Notice how the topic statement above used the same organization and vocabulary as the prompt.

Using the spaces provided below, form an opinion that responds to the prompt, and then rephrase your opinion to form a topic statement.

1)

Prompt

To whom do you usually go when you want advice regarding a problem or a difficult situation?

- Opinion: ______________________________

- Topic Statement: ______________________________

____

2)

Prompt

Describe one of your earliest memories. Why is it important to you?

- Opinion: ______________________________

- Topic Statement: ______________________________

____

3)

Prompt

What famous person have you frequently admired?

- Opinion: ______________________________

- Topic Statement: ______________________________

____

STEP 2B. PREPARE YOUR RESPONSE

ADDING REASONS AND DETAILS

Once you have composed a topic statement, you must be able to support your statement using **reasons.** While the topic statement tells the reader what your response to the prompt is, the reasons you choose tell the reader *why* you have chosen this particular topic statement.

When preparing your response, do not use full sentences to write down your reasons; just write down essential information that you can turn into a full response later.

Prompt

What is one skill or lesson that you have learned from the Internet rather than from school? Use specific reasons and details to support your answer.

- Topic Statement: *One skill I learned from the Internet was how to treat a sore throat.*

During your preparation time, write down the key points that you can expand upon in your response.

- Notes containing Reasons and Details
  - Detail 1: *had cold, no med.*
  - Detail 2: *search "sore throat," salt water*

Note Make sure that the reasons you come up with relate to your topic sentence. Getting off-topic in your response will make your response less coherent and lower your score.

Either review your topic sentences from the previous practice, or come up with new topic sentences to the prompts below. Then write down two reasons that support your topic statement in a note format.

1) **Prompt**

To whom do you usually go when you want advice regarding a problem or a difficult situation? Describe this person, and explain why you seek his or her advice.

- Topic Statement: ______________________________

____

- Notes
  - Reason 1: ______________________________
  - Reason 2: ______________________________

2) **Prompt**

Describe one of your earliest memories. Why is it important to you? Use specific reasons and details to support your answer.

- Topic Statement: ______________________________

____

- Notes
  - Reason 1: ______________________________
  - Reason 2: ______________________________

3) **Prompt**

What famous person have you frequently admired? Use specific reasons and examples to support your answer.

- Topic Statement: ______________________________

____

- Notes
  - Reason 1: ______________________________
  - Reason 2: ______________________________

STEP 3. DELIVER YOUR RESPONSE

Prompt

What is one skill or lesson that you have learned from the Internet rather than from school? Use specific reasons and details to support your answer.

- The first sentence of your response should present your opinion in the form of a **topic statement.**
- Give **two reasons** that support your topic statement. Use any notes you have for guidance, but make sure that you respond using complete sentences.
- When you respond, include **transition words** where they are appropriate. Doing so will clarify the relationships between ideas. See below for a sample of a completed response.

Example Response

	Notes		Response
Topic Statement	*treat sore throat*	➡	*One skill I learned from the Internet was how to treat a sore throat.*
Reason 1	*had cold, no med.*	➡	*During my first year in the dormitories at college, I developed a bad cold one night. It was too late at night to go to the store, and neither I nor my roommate had any cold medicine.*
Reason 2	*search "sore throat," salt water*	➡	*I searched the Internet using the words "sore throat," and found a couple of Internet sites that suggested gargling with warm, salty water. The salt helps shrink swollen tissues. I followed the directions, and they helped me feel better. It was great to being able to access the information that I needed.*

Following the steps below, develop a Task 1 response to the following prompt.

1) **Prompt**

To whom do you usually go when you want advice regarding a problem or a difficult situation? Describe this person, and explain why you seek his or her advice.

- Opinion: ______________________________

- Topic Statement: ______________________________

____

- Reason 1: ______________________________
- Reason 2: ______________________________

Now that you have created an outline, write down a full-length response. Once you have written down your response, **say it aloud to yourself, a friend, a classmate, or a family member**.

Response

____

Following the steps below, develop a Task 1 response to the following prompt.

1) **Prompt**

Describe one of your earliest memories. Why is it important to you? Use specific reasons and details to support your answer.

- Opinion: ______________________________

- Topic Statement: ______________________________

____

- Reason 1: ______________________________
- Reason 2: ______________________________

Now that you have created an outline, write down a full-length response. Once you have written down your response, **say it aloud to yourself, a friend, a classmate, or a family member**.

Response

____

____

____

____

____

____

____

____

____

____

____

____

Following the steps below, develop a Task 1 response to the following prompt.

1)

Prompt

What famous person have you frequently admired? Use specific reasons and examples to support your answer.

- Opinion: ____________________

- Topic Statement: ____________________

____

  - Reason 1: ____________________
  - Reason 2: ____________________

Now that you have created an outline, write down a full-length response. Once you have written down your response, **say it aloud to yourself, a friend, a classmate, or a family member**.

Response

____

____

____

____

____

____

____

____

____

____

____

____

EXERCISE 1

Following the steps below, develop a Task 1 response to the following prompt.

STEP 1. OUTLINE YOUR RESPONSE

Prompt

Name one national or world event in your lifetime that has affected you. Describe how this event has changed your life or your thinking. Use specific reasons and examples to support your answer.

- Opinion: ______________________________

STEP 2. PREPARE YOUR RESPONSE

00:00:15

- Topic Statement: ______________________________

  ____

  - Reason 1: ______________________________
  - Reason 2: ______________________________

STEP 3. DELIVER YOUR RESPONSE

00:00:45

Response

____

____

____

____

____

____

____

Now practice saying your response aloud. If possible, have a friend or a classmate fill out this checklist as you say your response to him or her. If you are by yourself, record and listen to your response, and then fill out the checklist below on your own.

Deliver your response within 45 seconds.

Task 1 Response Checklist

	Yes	Somewhat	No
• Does the speaker give his or her opinion in a topic statement?			
• Does the speaker support his or her opinion with at least two details or reasons?			
• Does the speaker deliver an organized response by using transition words and proper sentence structures?			
• Does the speaker deliver a coherent response by using appropriate tone and pronunciation?			
• Does the speaker finish within the time limit?		X	

EXERCISE 2

Following the steps below, develop a Task 1 response to the following prompt.

STEP 1. OUTLINE YOUR RESPONSE

Prompt

Who is the most adventurous person that you know? Explain what qualities make this person adventurous. Use specific details and examples to support your response.

- Opinion: ______________________________

STEP 2. PREPARE YOUR RESPONSE

00:00:15

- Topic Statement: ______________________________

____

  - Reason 1: ______________________________
  - Reason 2: ______________________________

STEP 3. DELIVER YOUR RESPONSE

00:00:45

Response

____

____

____

____

____

____

____

Now practice saying your response aloud. If possible, have a friend or a classmate fill out this checklist as you say your response to him or her. If you are by yourself, record and listen to your response, and then fill out the checklist below on your own.

Deliver your response within 45 seconds.

Task 1 Response Checklist

	Yes	Somewhat	No
• Does the speaker give his or her opinion in a topic statement?			
• Does the speaker support his or her opinion with at least two details or reasons?			
• Does the speaker deliver an organized response by using transition words and proper sentence structures?			
• Does the speaker deliver a coherent response by using appropriate tone and pronunciation?			
• Does the speaker finish within the time limit?		X	

EXERCISE 3

Following the steps below, develop a Task 1 response to the following prompt.

STEP 1. OUTLINE YOUR RESPONSE

Prompt

Life is different for every *generation* (people in the same age group). How is your generation's lifestyle different from your parents' lifestyle? Use specific reasons and examples to support your answer.

- Opinion: ______________________________

STEP 2. PREPARE YOUR RESPONSE

00:00:15

- Topic Statement: ______________________________

____

  - Reason 1: ______________________________
  - Reason 2: ______________________________

STEP 3. DELIVER YOUR RESPONSE

00:00:45

Response

____

____

____

____

____

____

____

Now practice saying your response aloud. If possible, have a friend or a classmate fill out this checklist as you say your response to him or her. If you are by yourself, record and listen to your response, and then fill out the checklist below on your own.

Deliver your response within 45 seconds.

Task 1 Response Checklist

	Yes	Somewhat	No
• Does the speaker give his or her opinion in a topic statement?			
• Does the speaker support his or her opinion with at least two details or reasons?			
• Does the speaker deliver an organized response by using transition words and proper sentence structures?			
• Does the speaker deliver a coherent response by using appropriate tone and pronunciation?			
• Does the speaker finish within the time limit?		╳	

MODEL ANSWER

EXERCISE 1

STEP 1. OUTLINE YOUR RESPONSE

- Opinion: *Curiosity rover → Mars (2012)*

STEP 2. PREPARE YOUR RESPONSE

- Topic Statement: *One event that greatly affected me was the landing of the Curiosity rover on the surface of Mars in 2012.*
  - Reason 1: *hope for human future*
  - Reason 2: *encouraged me to attend univ.*

STEP 3. DELIVER YOUR RESPONSE

One event that greatly affected me was the landing of the Curiosity rover on the surface of Mars in 2012. ***The first reason*** *this event affected me is that it gave me more hope for humanity's future. Sometimes it seems like all news is about pollution, crime, and corrupt politics, so reading about people cooperating to explore a distant planet made me feel optimistic and inspired. Seeing the Curiosity land on Mars also encouraged me to work harder in high school so that I could attend a university and become a part of future space missions.*

EXERCISE 2

STEP 1. OUTLINE YOUR RESPONSE

- Opinion: *my dad = adventurous*

STEP 2. PREPARE YOUR RESPONSE

- Topic Statement: *The most adventurous person I know is probably my dad. He loves traveling, but there are two reasons my dad is not just a traveler, but an adventurer.*
  - Reason 1: *travel → backpacking, skiing*
  - Reason 2: *spontaneous*

STEP 3. Deliver Your Response

The most adventurous person I know is probably my dad. He loves traveling, but there are two reasons my dad's not just a traveler, but an adventurer. ***First****, he goes to a lot of different kinds of places. He goes backpacking and skiing in the mountains, boards international flights to faraway places such as Siberia, and even just drives an hour to a city near his home to see plays and concerts.* ***Also****, when he travels with others, he doesn't plan everything ahead of time, so he's able to be spontaneous and do what his traveling companions want to do.* ***Therefore****, my dad is adventurous because he tries new things and is open to the unexpected.*

EXERCISE 3

STEP 1. Outline Your Response

- Opinion: *manual → digital labor*

STEP 2. Prepare Your Response

- Topic Statement: *The biggest lifestyle difference for my generation is that my parents had to work by hand at tasks that we complete digitally.*
  - Reason 1: *research: parents → long, now → quick*
  - Reason 2: *fun: parents → inconvenient, now → convenient*

STEP 3. Deliver Your Response

The biggest lifestyle difference for my generation is that my parents had to work by hand at tasks that we complete digitally. ***For example****, when my parents were students, they had to find information for reports in books, encyclopedias, or magazines. That meant going to the library for hours; we can get information we need from our iPhones or laptops in a few minutes.* ***Moreover****, having fun was also less convenient for my parents.* ***For example****, if people from my parents' generation wanted to play video games, they had to go to a video game room, and they could only play until their coins ran out. If they wanted to call home, they often had to make sure they had enough coins to use a pay phone. My generation is lucky to have digital technology that makes life more convenient.*

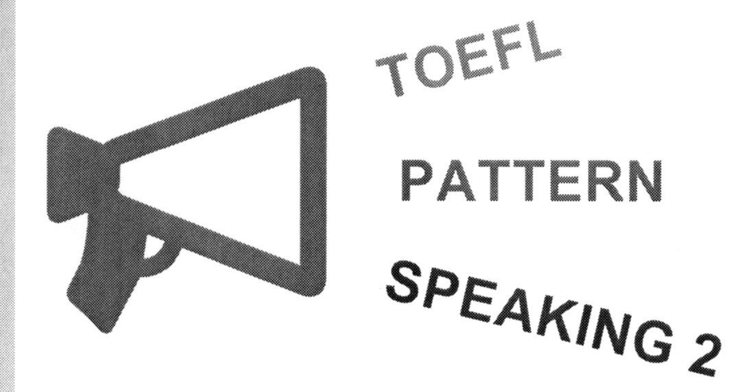

Task 2

CHAPTER 2

Selecting a Preference

Selecting a Preference

GENERAL BACKGROUND INFORMATION

1. EXPLANATION OF TASK 2

The prompt will present two possible actions, situations, or opinions. Choose which one of the two options you prefer, and then explain your preference with reasons and details. A narrator will read the prompt aloud; the prompt will stay on the computer screen during your preparation and response time.

You will then have 15 seconds to prepare your response. Begin preparing when the "Preparation Time" notice appears on your screen. Use the time to write down a few notes in outline form because you will not have enough time to write a full answer.

At the end of 15 seconds, you will hear a short beep. The "Preparation Time" notice changes to "Response Time." The countdown from 45 seconds begins. Your response will be recorded during the 45 seconds. At the end, the recording will stop. A new screen will indicate that the response time has ended.

2. NECESSARY SKILLS FOR TASK 2

You must be able to:

- take a position and support the position with reasons
- organize ideas coherently with a clear topic statement and supporting reasons
- speak clearly using correct grammar, vocabulary, and pronunciation

3. EXPLANATION OF QUESTION TYPES

The question will always ask that you respond with your preference and give reasons for your response. Your score is not based upon your preference but on how well you explain your preference.

Question Types

1 Picking a Preference about a University Issue

Some students prefer X (first university-related preference). Other students prefer Y (second university-related preference). Which do you prefer, and why? Use specific reasons and examples to support your answer.

2 Picking a Lifestyle or Ethical Preference

Some people believe X (first lifestyle/ethical preference). Other people believe Y (second lifestyle/ethical preference). Which opinion do you agree with, and why? Use specific details and examples to support your preference.

4. EXAMPLE PROMPTS

Possible Task 2 prompts that you may encounter on the official TOEFL exam include:

Prompt

- Some students prefer to attend universities in big cities while others choose small towns for their higher education. Support your answer with reasons.
- Some people appreciate advice from family, friends, and mentors. Others prefer to rely on their own experiences and learn through their own mistakes. Which method of learning do you prefer and why? Give reasons and details to support your answer.
- Do you agree or disagree with the following statement? It is easier to be a teacher than to be a student. Include reasons and details to support your answer.
- Some people try to perform several tasks at once while others prefer to concentrate on one specific task at a time. Which approach do you think is more effective and why? Use reasons and details to support your answer.
- Do you agree or disagree with the following statement? The most important lesson in life is learned outside the classroom. Use specific reasons and details to support your answer.

5. USEFUL EXPRESSIONS

Some useful expressions for Task 2 are:

- In my opinion, __________.
- I agree (that) __________ because __________.
- I disagree (that) __________ because __________.
- I prefer __________ to __________ because __________.
  (noun / noun phrase) *(noun / noun phrase)*
- I prefer to __________ than to __________ because __________.
  (verb / verb phrase) *(verb / verb phrase)*
- I think (that) __________ is better than __________ because __________.
- I believe (that) __________ is preferable to __________ because __________.
- Given the choice between __________ and __________, I prefer __________ because __________.

HACKING STRATEGY

STEP 1. OUTLINE YOUR RESPONSE

- Read the prompt carefully
- Decide on a preference

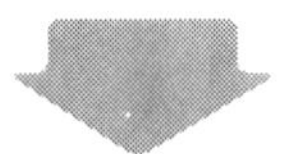

STEP 2. PREPARE YOUR RESPONSE

- Make your opinion into a topic statement
- Add reasons that support your preference

STEP 3. DELIVER YOUR RESPONSE

- Respond using coherent sentences
- Add transition words between ideas

EXAMPLE

STEP 1. OUTLINE YOUR RESPONSE

First, you must read the prompt carefully. Make sure that you understand exactly what the prompt is asking you to do.

Prompt

When attending a university, some students prefer to focus on one subject while others prefer to study many different subjects. Which do you prefer? Use specific reasons and details to explain why you have this preference.

For this prompt, the first thing you must decide is whether you prefer to study one subject or many subjects. Your response to the main part of the prompt is called your *preference*. After reading the prompt, quickly write down your preference. Make sure that you choose something you can support with reasons.

- Preference: *many subjects*

STEP 2. PREPARE YOUR RESPONSE

When organizing your response, you should make your preference into a topic statement and come up with at least two reasons or details that support your topic statement. Because you are only given 15 seconds to prepare for your response, you must organize your thoughts quickly.

- Topic Statement: *While there are many benefits to focusing on one subject during one's college career, I would prefer to study as many subjects as possible.*
  - Reason 1: *pursue interests/no burn-out*
  - Reason 2: *diff. ways of looking at things*

STEP 3. DELIVER YOUR RESPONSE

Use the outline that you created in STEP 2 to guide you as you deliver your response. Respond using complete sentences, and add transition words to show how ideas relate to one another.

While there are many benefits to focusing on one subject in college, I'd prefer to study as many subjects as possible. One reason is that I have many interests, so if I had to focus on just one subject, I might become bored with it. ***Also****, studying a wide range of subjects gives me many opportunities to consider new perspectives, which can be helpful when I'm studying or working.*

STEP 1. OUTLINE YOUR RESPONSE

▶ APPROACHING A PROMPT

Make sure that you respond to the entire prompt. One prompt will often ask you to address multiple points.

Prompt

Some people enjoy jobs that bring them into contact with the public, such as sales. Other people prefer jobs in which they mostly work alone, such as desk jobs. Which do you prefer and why? Use specific reasons and details to support your answer.

This prompt is instructing you to address three related points. You are being asked to:

1) identify your preferred type of job
2) state why you have this preference

Additionally, the prompt will always tell you to use *specific* reasons, details, and/or examples.

▶ SELECTING A PREFERENCE

All Task 2 prompts ask you to select one of two options. Because you only have 15 seconds to outline your entire response, deciding upon a preference quickly is crucial.

Prompt

Some people enjoy jobs that bring them into contact with the public, such as sales. Other people prefer jobs in which they mostly work alone, such as desk jobs. Which do you prefer and why?

Make sure that you select the preference that you feel comfortable talking about for 45 seconds. And remember, you are being scored based on how well you defend your preference, not based on which particular preference you select.

Because you should decide on your preference immediately after reading the prompt, use short phrases to state your opinion.

- Preference: *working alone*

Quickly choose a preference, and then give a reason that supports your selection.

1) Do you prefer to relax at home or seek adventure?

I prefer to *seek adventure* because *I become bored when I have too much free time*.

2) Would you prefer to live in an urban or rural area?

I would prefer to live in ________________ because ________________________________.

3) Would you rather read a book or watch a movie?

I would rather ________________ because ________________________________.

4) Do you prefer to stay up late at night or wake up early in the morning?

I prefer to ________________ because ________________________________.

PRACTICE 2

Write a brief phrase expressing your preference in response to each prompt.

1) **Prompt**

Explain why you agree or disagree with the following statement: it is better to get enough sleep before a test than to study all night.

- Preference: ________________________________

2) **Prompt**

What quality do you feel is more important when buying a car: fuel efficiency or engine performance?

- Preference: ________________________________

3) **Prompt**

Some instructors allow students to use electronics, such as laptops, during class. Other instructors prohibit the use of any electronics in class. Which rule do you prefer and why?

- Preference: ________________________________

STEP 2A. PREPARE YOUR RESPONSE

FORMING A TOPIC STATEMENT

The **topic statement** should be the first sentence of your speaking response. It gives your preference in the form of a statement. Make sure that you choose a preference that you can support with reasons and details for 45 seconds.

Create a topic statement by including vocabulary from the prompt to provide a clear and concise response to the prompt.

Prompt

Some people enjoy jobs that bring them into contact with the public, such as sales. Other people prefer jobs in which they mostly work alone, such as desk jobs. Which do you prefer and why?

- Preference: *working alone*

- Topic Statement: *While some people enjoy jobs that regularly bring them into contact with the public, I prefer jobs in which I work alone most of the time.*

Note Notice how the topic statement above used the same organization and vocabulary as the prompt.

Either review your preferences from the previous practice or come up with new preferences to the prompts below. Then use your preference to formulate a topic sentence for each prompt.

1) **Prompt**

Explain why you agree or disagree with the following statement: it is better to get enough sleep before a test than to study all night.

- Preference: ____________________

- Topic Statement: ____________________

____

2) **Prompt**

What quality do you feel is more important when buying a car: fuel efficiency or engine performance?

- Preference: ____________________

- Topic Statement: ____________________

____

3) **Prompt**

Some instructors allow students to use electronics, such as laptops, during class. Other instructors prohibit the use of any electronics in class. Which rule do you prefer and why?

- Preference: ____________________

- Topic Statement: ____________________

____

STEP 2B. PREPARE YOUR RESPONSE

ADDING REASONS AND DETAILS

Once you have composed a topic statement, you must be able to support your statement using reasons and/or details. While the topic statement tells the reader what your response to the prompt is, the reasons and details that you choose tell the reader why you have chosen this particular topic statement.

When preparing your response, do not use full sentences to write down your reasons; just write down essential information that you can turn into a full response later.

Prompt

Some people enjoy jobs that bring them into contact with the public, such as sales. Other people prefer jobs in which they mostly work alone, such as desk jobs. Which do you prefer and why? Use specific reasons and details to support your answer.

- Topic Statement: *While some people enjoy jobs that regularly bring them into contact with the public, I prefer jobs in which I work alone most of the time.*

During your preparation time, write down notes that you can expand upon in your response.

- Notes containing Reasons and Details
  - Reason 1: *peaceful/↑energy later*
  - Reason 2: *focus on 1 task/no interruptions*

Note Make sure that the reasons you come up with relate to your topic sentence. Getting off-topic in your response will make your response less coherent and lower your score.

Using your topic statement from the previous exercise, write down two reasons that support your topic statement in a brief note format.

1)

Prompt

Explain why you agree or disagree with the following statement: it is better to get enough sleep before a test than to study all night. Use specific reasons and details to support your answer.

- Topic Statement: ______________________________

____

▶ Notes

- Reason 1: ______________________________
- Reason 2: ______________________________

2)

Prompt

What quality do you feel is more important when buying a car: fuel efficiency or engine performance? Use specific reasons and details to support your answer.

- Topic Statement: ______________________________

____

▶ Notes

- Reason 1: ______________________________
- Reason 2: ______________________________

3)

Prompt

Some instructors allow students to use electronics, such as laptops, during class. Other instructors prohibit the use of any electronics in class. Which rule do you prefer and why? Use specific reasons and details to support your answer.

- Topic Statement: ______________________________

____

▶ Notes

- Reason 1: ______________________________
- Reason 2: ______________________________

STEP 3. DELIVER YOUR RESPONSE

Now you have all the pieces of information you need to deliver your response.

Prompt

Some people enjoy jobs that bring them into contact with the public, such as sales. Other people prefer jobs in which they mostly work alone, such as desk jobs. Which do you prefer and why? Use specific reasons and details to support your answer.

- The first sentence of your response should present your preference in the form of a **topic statement.**
- Then give the **two reasons** that support your topic statement. Use any notes that you have for guidance, but make sure that you respond using complete sentences.
- When you respond, include **transition words** where they are appropriate. Doing so will clarify the relationships between ideas. See below for a sample of a completed response.

Example Response

	Notes		Response
Preference	*working alone*	➡	*While some people enjoy jobs that regularly bring them into contact with the public, I prefer jobs that allow me to work alone most of the time.*
Reason 1	*peaceful/↑ energy later*	➡	***First**, a peaceful, quiet job leaves me less tired than one with a lot of interaction. **As a result**, I have more energy later for my own social life and personal plans.*
Reason 2	*focus on 1 task/no interruptions*	➡	***Moreover**, I'm the kind of person who likes to focus on one task at a time. I find interruptions stressful, whereas finishing a task gives me a feeling of accomplishment. **For that reason**, working alone at a desk job would be ideal for someone with my personality.*

Following the steps below, develop a Task 2 response to the following prompt.

1) **Prompt**

Explain why you agree or disagree with the following statement: it is better to get enough sleep before a test than to study all night. Use specific reasons and details to support your answer.

- Preference: ______________________________

- Topic Statement: ______________________________

____

  - Reason 1: ______________________________
  - Reason 2: ______________________________

Now that you have created an outline, write down a full-length response. Once you have written down your response, **say it aloud to yourself, a friend, a classmate, or a family member**.

Response

____

____

____

____

____

____

____

____

____

____

____

____

Following the steps below, develop a Task 2 response to the following prompt.

1) **Prompt**

What quality do you feel is more important when buying a car: fuel efficiency or engine performance? Use specific reasons and details to support your answer.

- Preference: ______________________________

- Topic Statement: ______________________________

____

  - Reason 1: ______________________________
  - Reason 2: ______________________________

Now that you have created an outline, write down a full-length response. Once you have written down your response, **say it aloud to yourself, a friend, a classmate, or a family member**.

Response

____

____

____

____

____

____

____

____

____

____

____

____

Following the steps below, develop a Task 2 response to the following prompt.

1)

Prompt

Some instructors allow students to use electronics, such as laptops, during class, while other instructors prohibit the use of any electronics in class. Which do you prefer and why? Use specific reasons and details to support your answer.

- Preference: ______________________________

- Topic Statement: ______________________________

____

  - Reason 1: ______________________________
  - Reason 2: ______________________________

Now that you have created an outline, write down a full-length response. Once you have written down your response, **say it aloud to yourself, a friend, a classmate, or a family member**.

Response

____

____

____

____

____

____

____

____

____

____

____

____

EXERCISE 1

Following the steps below, develop a response to the following prompt.

STEP 1. OUTLINE YOUR RESPONSE

Prompt

Explain why you agree or disagree with the following statement: high school students should be required to attend classes that teach them about proper etiquette. Use specific reasons and details to support your answer.

- Preference: ______________________________

STEP 2. PREPARE YOUR RESPONSE

00:00:15

- Topic Statement: ______________________________

____

  - Reason 1: ______________________________
  - Reason 2: ______________________________

STEP 3. DELIVER YOUR RESPONSE

00:00:45

Response

____

____

____

____

____

____

____

Now practice saying your response aloud. If possible, have a friend/classmate fill out this checklist as you say your response to him or her. If you are by yourself, record and listen to your response, and then fill out the checklist below on your own.

Deliver your response within 45 seconds.

Task 2 Response Checklist

	Yes	Somewhat	No
• Does the speaker give his or her preference in a topic statement?			
• Does the speaker support his or her preference with at least two details or reasons?			
• Does the speaker deliver an organized response by using transition words and proper sentence structures?			
• Does the speaker deliver a coherent response by using appropriate tone and pronunciation?			
• Does the speaker finish within the time limit?		X	

EXERCISE 2

Following the steps below, develop a response to the following prompt.

STEP 1. Outline Your Response

Prompt

Some students prefer to be graded mainly on projects and written reports, while other students prefer to be graded mainly on quizzes and tests. Which do you prefer and why? Use specific examples and details to support your answer.

- Preference: ____________________

STEP 2. Prepare Your Response

00:00:15

- Topic Statement: ____________________
  ____
  - Reason 1: ____________________
  - Reason 2: ____________________

STEP 3. Deliver Your Response

00:00:45

Response

____

____

____

____

____

____

____

Now practice saying your response aloud. If possible, have a friend/classmate fill out this checklist as you say your response to him or her. If you are by yourself, record and listen to your response, and then fill out the checklist below on your own.

Deliver your response within 45 seconds.

Task 2 Response Checklist

	Yes	Somewhat	No
• Does the speaker give his or her preference in a topic statement?			
• Does the speaker support his or her preference with at least two details or reasons?			
• Does the speaker deliver an organized response by using transition words and proper sentence structures?			
• Does the speaker deliver a coherent response by using appropriate tone and pronunciation?			
• Does the speaker finish within the time limit?		X	

EXERCISE 3

Following the steps below, develop a response to the following prompt.

STEP 1. OUTLINE YOUR RESPONSE

Prompt

Some people believe that additional government funding should go toward protecting the environment, while others believe that this funding should go toward space research and exploration. Which of these two projects do you believe the government should fund more? Use specific reasons and details to support your answer.

- Preference: ______________________________

STEP 2. PREPARE YOUR RESPONSE

00:00:15

- Topic Statement: ______________________________

____

  - Reason 1: ______________________________
  - Reason 2: ______________________________

STEP 3. DELIVER YOUR RESPONSE

00:00:45

Response

____

____

____

____

____

____

____

Now practice saying your response aloud. If possible, have a friend/classmate fill out this checklist as you say your response to him or her. If you are by yourself, record and listen to your response, and then fill out the checklist below on your own.

Deliver your response within 45 seconds.

Task 2 Response Checklist

	Yes	Somewhat	No
• Does the speaker give his or her preference in a topic statement?			
• Does the speaker support his or her preference with at least two details or reasons?			
• Does the speaker deliver an organized response by using transition words and proper sentence structures?			
• Does the speaker deliver a coherent response by using appropriate tone and pronunciation?			
• Does the speaker finish within the time limit?		X	

EXERCISE 1

STEP 1. OUTLINE YOUR RESPONSE

- Preference: *no etiquette classes in school*

STEP 2. PREPARE YOUR RESPONSE

- Topic Statement: *I don't believe that schools should take time out of academic class schedules to offer etiquette classes for a number of reasons.*
  - Reason 1: *schools → enough responsibility*
  - Reason 2: *manners should be taught @ home*

STEP 3. DELIVER YOUR RESPONSE

I don't believe that schools should take time out of academic class schedules to offer etiquette classes for a number of reasons. ***For one****, schools should focus on teaching students about academic subjects. Because most schools already have a hard time fitting all necessary academic classes into their schedules, they should not try to add any extra, non-academic classes.* ***Additionally****, every family has different ideas about what's polite versus what's impolite.* ***As a result****, etiquette should be taught at home rather than in school.*

EXERCISE 2

STEP 1. OUTLINE YOUR RESPONSE

- Preference: *grades → projects & writing*

STEP 2. PREPARE YOUR RESPONSE

- Topic Statement: *When choosing a preferred grading method, I would rather be graded based on projects and written reports than based on test and quiz scores.*
  - Reason 1: *control outcome of project*
  - Reason 2: *writing = more critical thinking*

STEP 3. DELIVER YOUR RESPONSE

When choosing a preferred grading method, I'd rather be graded based on projects and written reports than on test and quiz scores. Because I never know exactly what material will be on a test, I never feel completely prepared for it. But when I work on a project, I can control exactly what information I want to present and how I want to present it. ***Moreover****, I enjoy writing papers because, unlike most tests and quizzes, written reports give me an opportunity to reflect on the material that I'm discussing, allowing for lots of critical thinking.* ***Overall****, I think critical thinking is much more important than the memorization necessary for most tests.*

EXERCISE 3

STEP 1. OUTLINE YOUR RESPONSE

- Preference: *$ toward env.*

STEP 2. PREPARE YOUR RESPONSE

- Topic Statement: *If the government had to choose between increasing funding for space exploration or environmental research, I believe that more money should be invested in the environment.*
  - Reason 1: *more immediate concern*
  - Reason 2: ↑ *knowledge of Earth* = ↑ *knowledge of space*

STEP 3. DELIVER YOUR RESPONSE

If the government had to choose between increasing funding for space exploration or environmental research, I believe that more money should be invested in the environment. ***For one****, preventing greenhouse gas emissions and water pollution is a more immediate concern than reaching distant planets. Our actions do more damage to the environment every day, so we should immediately research ways to stop and even reverse the harm that human activities have caused.* ***Also****, focusing on more efficient forms of energy production to help the environment can also help us master space travel in the future, so fixing the Earth might actually help us leave it, too.*

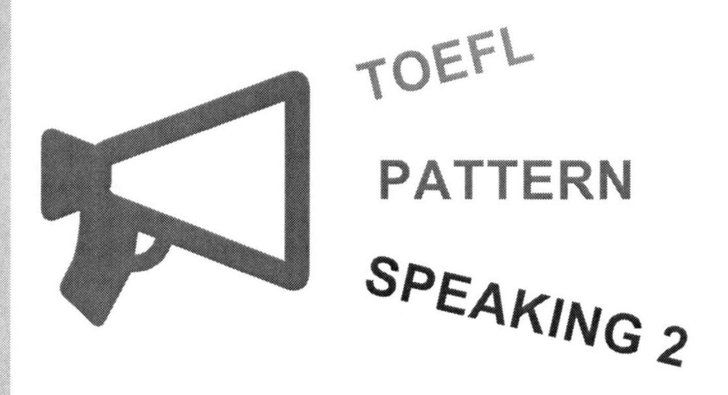

CHAPTER 3

Campus Situation

(Reading and Listening)

Campus Situation

GENERAL BACKGROUND INFORMATION

1. EXPLANATION OF TASK 3

Task 3 requires that you read a brief announcement of 75 to 100 words about a change on campus; the reading may be presented in the form of a newspaper article or a campus-wide notification. You will be given 45 to 50 seconds to read the announcement. Common topics include:

- building, updating, or improving structures on campus
- creating and enforcing new campus rules and regulations
- changing admission, registration, or graduation requirements

The announcement presents information about a proposed change to campus, including two or more reasons for this change.

After reading the announcement, you will listen to two students discuss the subject presented in the announcement. One speaker will either strongly support or oppose the change. The conversation is 60 to 80 seconds long.

After the conversation ends, you will be given a prompt related to what you have read and heard. The prompt appears on your computer screen and is read aloud by a narrator.

Prompt

The man/woman expresses his/her opinion about the plan described in the announcement. Briefly summarize the plan. Then state his/her opinion about the plan and explain the reasons he/she gives for holding that opinion.

After seeing the prompt, you have 30 seconds to prepare your response. At the end, you will hear a short beep. The clock then changes to "Response Time" and begins to count down.

You have 60 seconds to respond. At the end of the 60 seconds, the recording ends and a new message alerts you that the response time is over.

You may take notes while reading, listening, and preparing. You also may check your notes when responding to the question.

2. NECESSARY SKILLS FOR TASK 3

You must be able to:

- understand information from written and spoken sources regarding campus-based subject matter
- identify and summarize major points and important details from written and spoken sources
- synthesize information from written and spoken sources

HACKING STRATEGY

STEP 1. OUTLINE YOUR RESPONSE

- Take notes as you read the announcement
- Take notes as you listen to the conversation
- Read the prompt carefully

STEP 2. PREPARE YOUR RESPONSE

- Summarize the university's announcement
- State the student's opinion regarding the announcement
- State the student's reasons for holding this opinion

STEP 3. DELIVER YOUR RESPONSE

- Respond using coherent sentences
- Add transition words between ideas

HACKING STRATEGY EXAMPLE

STEP 1. OUTLINE YOUR RESPONSE

Take notes on essential information as you read the university's announcement and listen to the conversation. Do not take notes using full sentences, as you will not have time to do so.

UNIVERSITY ANNOUNCEMENT

New Radio Station

The university is pleased to announce that it will open a radio broadcast station on campus next spring. The station will broadcast news and educational programs produced by a professional staff. It will also air news from National Public Radio.

University officials expect that the station will provide a public service to the community surrounding the campus because it will offer independent, in-depth radio news. The station will also provide internship opportunities for the university's students, allowing them to learn about radio technology and journalism.

CONVERSATION

M: *Did you hear about the new radio station they're putting in?*

F: *Yeah, I did. I can't wait!*

M: *Really? Why? Having a station that focuses on the news sounds so boring.*

F: *Well, a lot of us should follow world news a little more closely. Now we'll have a really high-quality news station to make it easier to keep ourselves a little, you know, informed.*

M: *I guess so.*

F: *I'm definitely going to apply for one of those internships. I think learning about the broadcasting industry would be fascinating.*

M: *(laughing) Okay, I'll catch up on the news when you're on air!*

M: *Male Student* / **F:** *Female Student*

ANNOUNCEMENT NOTES

Proposal: *new radio station w/ N.P.R.*

- **Reason 1:** *public service, in-depth news*
- **Reason 2:** *opportunities for students (intern)*

CONVERSATION NOTES

Speaker's opinion: *woman supports*

- **Reason 1:** *students → more informed*
- **Reason 2:** *wants internship, interest in broadcast*

Once you have taken notes on the passage and the lecture, carefully read the prompt.

Prompt

The woman expresses her opinion about the plan described in the announcement. Briefly summarize the plan. Then state her opinion about the plan and explain the reasons she gives for holding that opinion.

STEP 2. PREPARE YOUR RESPONSE

During the 30-second preparation time, make sure that your notes address all the points in the prompt, and use the information in your notes to organize your response. Because you have so little time to prepare your response, do not write complete sentences.

1) Make sure that you can summarize the university's proposal.
   From Notes → Proposal: *new radio station w/ N.P.R*

2) Make sure that you know whether the speaker supports or opposes the proposal.
   From Notes → Speaker's opinion: *woman supports*

3) Make sure that you know why the student either supports or opposes the proposal.
   From Notes → Reason 1: *students → more informed*
   → Reason 2: *wants internship, interest in broadcast*

STEP 3. DELIVER YOUR RESPONSE

Use the outline that you created in STEP 2 to guide you as you deliver your response. Respond using complete sentences, and add transition words to show how ideas relate to one another.

In the announcement, the university explains its reasons for opening a new radio broadcasting station on campus. The station will broadcast news and information, including news programs from National Public Radio. The woman's enthusiastic about the planned radio station. She agrees with the university's claim that the station can provide an important public service by airing high-quality news programs. The woman says that the community surrounding the campus will benefit, and that the students will also become informed about the world. The woman also supports the university's goal of providing student internships at the station. In fact, she says she'll apply for one because she finds the idea of working in broadcasting to be "fascinating."

STEP 1A. OUTLINE YOUR RESPONSE

NOTE-TAKING STRATEGIES

Taking notes quickly during the reading and listening portions of this task is crucial, as you can use your notes to help outline your speaking response. When taking notes, you should be able to **abbreviate**, or shorten, common words or phrases and **condense information** in order to save time.

Tips for taking notes

- Only write down key points/information that you will use in your response.
- Because of time constraints, do not write using full sentences.
- Make sure that you can understand your own abbreviations.

TAKING NOTES ON THE UNIVERSITY ANNOUNCEMENT

The passage will present a university-related announcement along with one or more reasons justifying the announcement. Therefore, successful notes will summarize the announcement and list the reasons for the change.

UNIVERSITY ANNOUNCEMENT

Bike Rental Program

The university's Student Association is launching a bike rental program beginning next week. Students with a valid student identification card will be able to rent a bicycle for 30 dollars a month. Renters will have to pay for the bike if it is lost or stolen.

Student Association President Alex Smith said that the idea behind the rental program is to encourage students to ride bicycles instead of driving cars to campus, as there is currently not enough parking for all students. "We hope to ease the parking problem on campus," Smith said. "And what is more convenient than jumping on a bike? We think students will love this program because it makes getting to class much easier."

ANNOUNCEMENT NOTES

Proposal: *Student Assoc. bike rental program, $30/month*

- **Reason 1:** *ease parking prob.*
- **Reason 2:** ↑ *convenient for students*

Read the university's announcement, and fill out the note template that follows.

UNIVERSITY ANNOUNCEMENT

Game Room Closure

University President Joan Lee has announced plans to close the video game room in the Student Union. The closure will be effective at the end of the month. "The video game room has become outdated, and the administrators have decided not to invest in new games," Lee said. "A very small number of students use the video game room currently." Lee said that the university will use the space to expand the adjacent bowling alley.

ANNOUNCEMENT NOTES

Proposal: ______________________________

- Reason 1: ______________________________

____

- Reason 2: ______________________________

____

STEP 1B. OUTLINE YOUR RESPONSE

TAKING NOTES ON THE CONVERSATION

The conversation will present one speaker who either supports or opposes the proposal. In your notes, you should identify the speaker's opinion and list the reasons that the speaker is taking this stance.

CONVERSATION

F: *So what do you think about this new bike rental thing? Are you gonna get one?*

M: *No way. I think the Student Association's making a big mistake.*

F: *Really? Why? I thought you loved cycling.*

M: *Oh, yeah, I do. I mean they're making a financial mistake. They bought all these bikes, and I don't think anyone is going to rent them.*

F: *So you think it'll be unpopular?*

M: *Yep. Look at it this way: why should anyone pay 30 dollars a month? It's a waste of money. After renting a bike for a full school year, you will have spent nearly as much as if you had just bought your own bicycle.*

F: *That's true. The price is pretty high for just renting. But it would be more convenient than trying to park a car here, like they say.*

M: *Yeah, it would be convenient, but only when the weather is nice. I mean, no one's gonna ride a bike to campus in the snow or rain. So those people would have to spend even more money to ride the bus when the weather is bad. It's just not worth it to pay that much to rent a bike.*

F: *Female Student* / **M:** *Male Student*

CONVERSATION NOTES

Speaker's opinion: *man opposes*

- **Reason 1:** *price high; waste of $ (buy own bike)*
- **Reason 2:** *bike → bad in snow, rain; $ for bus*

The following conversation corresponds with the announcement from the previous page. Read the conversation, and fill out the note template that follows.

CONVERSATION

M: *So, are you mad about the announcement?*

F: *About the game room? Nah, not really. Closing it is probably a good thing.*

M: *Really? But I thought you loved playing video games.*

F: *I mean, I love gaming, but these days nobody needs those old-fashioned video game rooms. That's like from my parents' era. Now, people mostly play games on the Internet.*

M: *Yeah, I guess you're right.*

F: *I mean, people still like to watch other people play or compete against each other, but you can do that online now. They even have online tournaments.*

M: *Male Student* / **F:** *Female Student*

CONVERSATION NOTES

Speaker's opinion: ______________________________

- Reason 1: ______________________________

____

- Reason 2: ______________________________

____

STEP 2. PREPARE YOUR RESPONSE

UNIVERSITY ANNOUNCEMENT

Bike Rental Program

The university's Student Association is launching a bike rental program beginning next week. Students with a valid student identification card will be able to rent a bicycle for 30 dollars a month. Renters will have to pay for the bike if it is lost or stolen.

Student Association President Alex Smith said that the idea behind the rental program is to encourage people to ride bicycles instead of drive cars to campus, as there is currently not enough parking for all students. "We hope to ease the parking problem on campus," Smith said. "And what is more convenient than jumping on a bike? We think students will love this program because it makes getting to class much easier."

CONVERSATION

F: *So what do you think about this new bike rental thing? Are you gonna get one?*

M: *No way. I think the Student Association's making a big mistake.*

F: *Really? Why? I thought you loved cycling.*

M: *Oh, yeah, I do. I think they're making a financial mistake. They bought all these bikes, and I don't think anyone is going to rent them.*

F: *So you think it'll be unpopular?*

M: *Yep. Look at it this way: why should anyone pay 30 dollars a month? It's a waste of money. After renting a bike for a full school year, you will have spent nearly as much as if you had just bought your own bicycle.*

F: *That's true. The price is pretty high for just renting. But it would be more convenient than trying to park a car here, like they say.*

M: *Yeah, it would be convenient, but only when the weather is nice. I mean, no one's gonna ride a bike to campus in the snow or rain. So those people would have to spend even more money to ride public transportation when the weather is bad. It's just not worth it to pay that much to rent a bike.*

ANNOUNCEMENT NOTES

Proposal: *Student Assoc. bike rental program, $30/month*

- **Reason 1:** *ease car parking prob.*
- **Reason 2:** *more convenient for students*

CONVERSATION NOTES

Speaker's opinion: *man opposes*

- **Reason 1:** *price high; waste of money (student could buy own bike)*
- **Reason 2:** *inconvenient in snow, rain; pay for pub. transp.*

Once you have finished listening to the conversation, the prompt will appear on the screen.

Prompt

The man expresses his opinion regarding the university's announcement. State his opinion and explain the reasons he gives for holding this opinion.

After reading the prompt, you have 30 seconds to prepare your response. During your preparation time, organize your notes so you can address the following pieces of information in your response.

1) Make sure that you can summarize the university's proposal.

From Notes → Proposal: *Student Association bike rental program, $30/month*

2) Make sure that you know whether the speaker supports or opposes the proposal.

From Notes → Speaker's opinion: *man opposes*

3) Make sure that you know why the student either supports or opposes the proposal.

From Notes → Reason 1: *price high; waste of money (student could buy own bike)*

Reason 2: *inconvenient in snow, rain; pay for public transportation*

Read the university's announcement and the conversation. Then prepare a Task 3 response, using the template below. Review your notes from the previous practices if necessary.

UNIVERSITY ANNOUNCEMENT

Game Room Closure

University President Joan Lee has announced plans to close the video game room in the Student Union. The closure will be effective at the end of the month. "The video game room has become outdated, and the administrators have decided not to invest in new games," Lee said. "A very small number of students use the video game room currently." Lee said that the university will use the space to expand the adjacent bowling alley.

CONVERSATION

M: *So, are you mad about the announcement?*

F: *About the game room? Nah, not really. Closing it is probably a good thing.*

M: *Really? But I thought you loved playing video games.*

F: *I mean, I love gaming, but these days nobody needs those old-fashioned video game rooms. That's like from my parents' era. Now, people mostly play games on the Internet.*

M: *Yeah, I guess you're right.*

F: *I mean, people still like to watch other people play or compete against each other, but you can do that online now. They even have online tournaments.*

M: *Male Student* / **F:** *Female Student*

Prompt

The woman expresses her opinion regarding the university's announcement. Briefly summarize the plan. State her opinion and explain the reasons she gives for holding this opinion.

1) What is the university's proposal?

From Notes → Proposal: ______________________________

2) Does the speaker support or oppose the proposal?

From Notes → Speaker's opinion: ______________________________

3) Why does the student either support or oppose the proposal?

From Notes → Reason 1: ______________________________

Reason 2: ______________________________

STEP 3. DELIVER YOUR RESPONSE

Use the outline that you created in STEP 2 to guide you as you respond to the prompt.

Prompt

The man expresses his opinion regarding the university's announcement. Briefly summarize the plan. State his opinion and explain the reasons he gives for holding this opinion.

- **Announcement Summary:** The first sentence of your response should be a summary of the university's announcement. If you have enough time during your response, explain why the university is making the campus changes that are described in the announcement.
- **Speaker's Opinion:** Then state whether the student agrees or disagrees with the university's announcement.
- **Reasons for Opinion:** Lastly, state the reasons the student gives for supporting or opposing the university's announcement.
- Include **transition words** in your response to clarify the relationships between related ideas.

Example Response

	Notes	Response
Announcement Summary	*Student Assoc. bike rental program, $30/ month*	*The university's Student Association has announced a plan to offer bicycles for rent on a monthly basis, mainly because parking's become a real problem on campus.*
Speaker's Opinion	*man opposes*	***However**, the man opposes the bike-rental plan, claiming that it's a bad financial decision that will be unpopular with students.*
Reasons for Opinion	*price high: waste of money (could buy own bike)*	***One reason** the rentals will be unpopular, according to the man, is the price. Students have no reason to rent a bike for a school year when they could buy a bike for about the same amount of money.*
	inconvenient in snow, rain; pay for pub. transp.	***Additionally**, the man predicts that students won't want to use bicycles when it's snowing or raining. They'd have to spend even more money to take the bus. **Thus**, he thinks that the students won't find the rental bicycles convenient enough to pay the monthly fee.*

Review the following university announcement, conversation, and prompt. Then write a Task 3 response. Review your notes from the previous practices if necessary. Once you have written down your response, **say it aloud to yourself, a friend, a classmate, or a family member**.

UNIVERSITY ANNOUNCEMENT

Game Room Closure

University President Joan Lee has announced plans to close the video game room in the Student Union. The closure will be effective at the end of the month. "The video game room has become outdated, and the administrators have decided not to invest in new games," Lee said. "A very small number of students use the video game room currently." Lee said that the university will use the space to expand the adjacent bowling alley.

CONVERSATION

M: *So, are you mad about the announcement?*

F: *About the game room? Nah, not really. Closing it is probably a good thing.*

M: *Really? But I thought you loved playing video games.*

F: *I mean, I love gaming, but these days nobody needs those old-fashioned video game rooms. That's like from my parents' era. Now, people mostly play games on the Internet.*

M: *Yeah, I guess you're right.*

F: *I mean, people still like to watch other people play or compete against each other, but you can do that online now. They even have online tournaments.*

M: *Male Student* / **F:** *Female Student*

Prompt

The woman expresses her opinion regarding the university's announcement. Briefly summarize the plan. State her opinion and explain the reasons she gives for holding this opinion.

Response

EXERCISE 1

Following the steps below, develop a response to the following prompt.

STEP 1. Outline Your Response

UNIVERSITY ANNOUNCEMENT

Change in Menu

Next semester, the university's dining service will begin Meatless Mondays. On Monday nights, dining halls throughout campus will serve a selection of vegetarian dishes from various cultures. The dining halls will not serve meat, including chicken or fish. One reason for Meatless Mondays is the environmental costs of raising animals for meat. For example, raising cattle for beef requires huge amounts of water and grain. Raising vegetables, beans, and grains requires fewer resources. Another reason for Meatless Mondays is a focus on nutrition. Simply put, plants tend to be higher in vitamins and fiber than meat is.

CONVERSATION

F: *Meatless Mondays? Oh, no, this sounds terrible.*
M: *What do you mean? I think it'll be great.*
F: *How can you say that? It sounds so dull, like it'll just be rice and beans.*
M: *Well, they said it'll come from different cultures. You know, curries, stews, roasted veggies, stir-fried dishes, things like that.*
F: *Mmm, that does sound good. I hope you're right. It could be kind of adventurous.*
M: *Sure, and it'll make people feel good about themselves, too.*
F: *Feel good about themselves?*
M: *Yeah, because they'll be eating something healthy, with all the vegetables and everything. Also, they'll feel like they're doing something "green" to save the planet.*
F: *Okay, I see what you mean. "Green," nutritious, and hopefully delicious! That will feel good.*

F: *Female Student* / **M:** *Male Student*

ANNOUNCEMENT NOTES

Proposal: ______________________________

____

- Reason 1: ______________________________

____

- Reason 2: ______________________________

____

CONVERSATION NOTES

Speaker's opinion: ______________________________

____

- Reason 1: ______________________________

____

- Reason 2: ______________________________

____

Prompt

The man expresses his opinion regarding the university's announcement. Briefly summarize the proposal. State his opinion and explain the reasons he gives for holding this opinion.

STEP 2. PREPARE YOUR RESPONSE

00:00:30

1) What is the university's proposal?

From Notes → Proposal: ______________________________

2) Does the speaker support or oppose the proposal?

From Notes → Speaker's opinion: ______________________________

3) Why does the student either support or oppose the proposal?

From Notes → Reason 1: ______________________________

Reason 2: ______________________________

STEP 3. DELIVER YOUR RESPONSE

00:01:00

Response

____

____

____

____

____

____

____

____

____

Now practice saying your response aloud. If possible, have a friend or a classmate fill out this checklist as you say your response to him or her. If you are by yourself, record and listen to your response, and then fill out the checklist below on your own.

Deliver your response within 60 seconds.

Task 3 Response Checklist

	Yes	Somewhat	No
• Does the speaker summarize the university's proposal?			
• Does the speaker state the student's opinion regarding the university's proposal?			
• Does the speaker list the student's two reasons for agreeing or disagreeing with the proposal?			
• Does the speaker deliver an organized response by using transition words and proper sentence structures?			
• Does the speaker deliver a coherent response by using appropriate tone and pronunciation?			
• Does the speaker finish within the time limit?		X	

ANNOUNCEMENT NOTES

Proposal: *dining hall = Meatless Monday*

- **Reason 1:** *"env. cost" of meat (H_2O, food for livestock)*
- **Reason 2:** *plants = ↑ nutrition than meat*

CONVERSATION NOTES

Speaker's opinion: *man supports*

- **Reason 1:** *try food from diff. cultures*
- **Reason 2:** *healthy & env. friendly food*

1) What is the university's proposal?

From Notes → Proposal: *dining hall = Meatless Monday*

2) Does the speaker support or oppose the proposal?

From Notes → Speaker's opinion: *man supports*

3) Why does the student either support or oppose the proposal?

From Notes → Reason 1: *try food from different cultures*

Reason 2: *healthy and environment friendly*

Response

The university announced that it will begin "Meatless Mondays" next semester, so the dining hall will offer only vegetarian dishes on Mondays. The man is in favor of this proposal for a couple of reasons. First, he says that it'll be exciting to try vegetarian food from different cultures. The man also says that Meatless Mondays will make people feel better about their health because vegetarian dishes are usually more nutritious than meat dishes. Finally, he agrees with the announcement that eating vegetarian dishes is better for the environment. He thinks that students will be excited to do something environmentally friendly.

EXERCISE 2

Following the steps below, develop a response to the following prompt.

STEP 1. Outline Your Response

UNIVERSITY ANNOUNCEMENT

Changing the School's Mascot

The university administration is proposing a new mascot to represent the school and its sports teams. It would like students to vote on changing the mascot, which is now a gray squirrel. The university will hold an election to see if students will approve of a wolf as the new mascot instead.

Although the squirrel is a cute and resourceful animal, it is not associated with tough competition. A mascot should serve as a fundamental symbol of the student body. Administrators believe that having a tough wolf as a mascot may increase school pride.

CONVERSATION

M: *Wow, can you believe that they wanna get rid of the gray squirrel?*

F: *No, I can't! How can they even suggest getting rid of our little tree rodent?*

M: *Yeah, I like how squirrels can run up tree trunks so fast.*

F: *I mean, nothing against wolves, but having a squirrel as a mascot is unique. It really makes our school stand out from the crowd. Tons of schools have wolf mascots, but I can't think of any other school that has the gray squirrel.*

M: *That's true. But don't you think we should have a mascot that is big or powerful animal?*

F: *Well, when you think about it, squirrels are kind of amazing. Think about how tough you have to be to crack open a nut or an acorn with just your teeth.*

M: *True. I guess they must be pretty strong.*

F: *And, like you said, they're very, very fast. So, tough and fast, that's a pretty good combination for any mascot, don't you think?*

M: *Male Student* / **F:** *Female Student*

ANNOUNCEMENT NOTES

Proposal: ______________________

____

- Reason 1: ______________________

____

- Reason 2: ______________________

____

CONVERSATION NOTES

Speaker's opinion: ______________________

____

- Reason 1: ______________________

____

- Reason 2: ______________________

____

Prompt

The woman expresses her opinion regarding the university's announcement. Briefly summarize the proposal. State her opinion and explain the reasons she gives for holding this opinion.

STEP 2. PREPARE YOUR RESPONSE

00:00:30

1) What is the university's proposal?

From Notes → Proposal: ______________________________

2) Does the speaker support or oppose the proposal?

From Notes → Speaker's opinion: ______________________________

3) Why does the student either support or oppose the proposal?

From Notes → Reason 1: ______________________________

Reason 2: ______________________________

STEP 3. DELIVER YOUR RESPONSE

00:01:00

Response

____

____

____

____

____

____

____

____

____

Now practice saying your response aloud. If possible, have a friend or a classmate fill out this checklist as you say your response to him or her. If you are by yourself, record and listen to your response, and then fill out the checklist below on your own.

Deliver your response within 60 seconds.

Task 3 Response Checklist

	Yes	Somewhat	No
• Does the speaker summarize the university's proposal?			
• Does the speaker state the student's opinion regarding the university's proposal?			
• Does the speaker list the student's two reasons for agreeing or disagreeing with the proposal?			
• Does the speaker deliver an organized response by using transition words and proper sentence structures?			
• Does the speaker deliver a coherent response by using appropriate tone and pronunciation?			
• Does the speaker finish within the time limit?		X	

ANNOUNCEMENT NOTES

Proposal: *new mascot, squirrel → wolf*

- **Reason 1:** *squirrel ≠ competition*
- **Reason 2:** *tough wolf ↑ school spirit*

CONVERSATION NOTES

Speaker's opinion: *woman opposes*

- **Reason 1:** *squirrel = unique, wolf = common*
- **Reason 2:** *squirrel = tough + fast*

1) What is the university's proposal?

From Notes → Proposal: *new mascot, squirrel → wolf*

2) Does the speaker support or oppose the proposal?

From Notes → Speaker's opinion: *woman opposes*

3) Why does the student either support or oppose the proposal?

From Notes → Reason 1: *squirrel = unique, wolf = common*

Reason 2: *squirrel = tough + fast*

Response

The university will hold an election to see if students are in favor of changing the school's mascot from a gray squirrel to a wolf, claiming that the squirrel's not a tough enough animal to have as a mascot. The female student opposes this proposal, and she gives two reasons for the school to keep its squirrel mascot. First, she believes that too many schools already use a wolf as their mascot. She likes the gray squirrel mascot because it is an unusual animal to have represent a university. Additionally, she states that squirrels are actually very quick and hardy. They can chew through hard acorns and race up trees, and she thinks that such an extraordinary animal makes a perfect school mascot.

EXERCISE 3

Following the steps below, develop a response to the following prompt.

STEP 1. OUTLINE YOUR RESPONSE

UNIVERSITY ANNOUNCEMENT

Volunteer Mentor Program

The counseling center will start offering a mentoring program for first-year students in the fall of next year. The program will pair older student volunteers with incoming freshmen who are looking for some guidance. Mentors will help by offering advice on how to make friends, how to handle academic challenges, and how to adjust to living away from home. The center will host monthly social gatherings for the mentors and mentees. Although the program will only be open to 100 freshman participants at first, the center hopes to expand the program as funding becomes available.

CONVERSATION

F: *So what are your thoughts on the new program at the counseling center?*

M: *I'm so glad they're starting that, it sounds really helpful.*

F: *Yeah, we could've used mentors when we were freshmen, right?*

M: *We sure could have! Because you don't really know anyone yet, those first few months are kind of hard. It makes sense to have a kind of "big brother" or "big sister" to help you figure out how to join things, to show you where people go to hang out, things like that. It could prevent people from dropping out.*

F: *That'd be great.*

M: *And It'll probably be a great experience for the older students who are mentoring, too. They'll feel like they're helping someone, and they can put it on their resumes when they apply for jobs.*

F: *Hey, it sounds like you've talked yourself into it.*

M: *You have a point there. I think I'll apply to be a volunteer mentor in the program.*

F: *Female Student* / **M:** *Male Student*

ANNOUNCEMENT NOTES

Proposal: ______________________

____

- Reason 1: ______________________

____

- Reason 2: ______________________

____

CONVERSATION NOTES

Speaker's opinion: ______________________

____

- Reason 1: ______________________

____

- Reason 2: ______________________

____

Prompt

The man expresses his opinion regarding the university's announcement. Briefly summarize the proposal. State his opinion and explain the reasons he gives for holding this opinion.

STEP 2. PREPARE YOUR RESPONSE

00:00:30

1) What is the university's proposal?

From Notes → Proposal: ____________________

2) Does the speaker support or oppose the proposal?

From Notes → Speaker's opinion: ____________________

3) Why does the student either support or oppose the proposal?

From Notes → Reason 1: ____________________

Reason 2: ____________________

STEP 3. DELIVER YOUR RESPONSE

00:01:00

Response

____

____

____

____

____

____

____

____

____

Now practice saying your response aloud. If possible, have a friend or a classmate fill out this checklist as you say your response to him or her. If you are by yourself, record and listen to your response, and then fill out the checklist below on your own.

Deliver your response within 60 seconds.

Task 3 Response Checklist

	Yes	Somewhat	No
• Does the speaker summarize the university's proposal?			
• Does the speaker state the student's opinion regarding the university's proposal?			
• Does the speaker list the student's two reasons for agreeing or disagreeing with the proposal?			
• Does the speaker deliver an organized response by using transition words and proper sentence structures?			
• Does the speaker deliver a coherent response by using appropriate tone and pronunciation?			
• Does the speaker finish within the time limit?		X	

ANNOUNCEMENT NOTES

Proposal: *next yr. → mentor program*

- **Reason 1:** *help f-men adjust to college life*
- **Reason 2:** *hold soc. gatherings*

CONVERSATION NOTES

Speaker's opinion: *man supports*

- **Reason 1:** *f-man yr. = hard adjustment period, social help good*
- **Reason 2:** *exp. for mentors → helpful; good for resume*

1) What is the university's proposal?

From Notes → Proposal: *mentor program: help freshmen adjust, socialize*

2) Does the speaker support or oppose the proposal?

From Notes → Speaker's opinion: *man supports*

3) Why does the student either support or oppose the proposal?

From Notes → Reason 1: *freshman year = hard adjustment period, social help good*

Reason 2: *experience for mentors → helpful; good for resume*

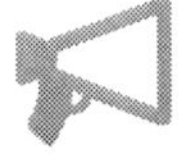

Response

Starting next year, the university will support a mentoring program where older college students will give freshmen advice about how to adjust to the social and academic challenges of college. The man in the conversation supports this proposal. He believes that the program will provide valuable guidance to incoming freshmen, and he says that the program might reduce college dropout rates by encouraging freshmen to be more involved in college life. Moreover, he claims that the experience will be good for the mentors, who'll get to improve their resumes while helping younger students. The man's so enthusiastic about the program that he says he'll sign up to be a mentor.

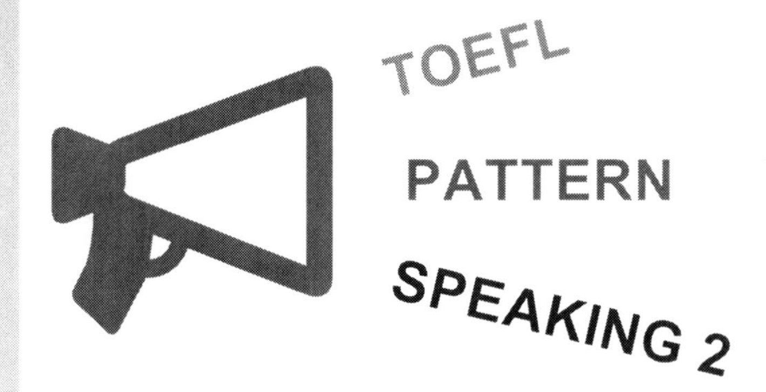

Task 4

CHAPTER 4

Academic Course

(Reading and Listening)

Academic Course

GENERAL BACKGROUND INFORMATION

1. EXPLANATION OF TASK 4

Speaking Task 4 requires that you connect the information in an academic reading passage to the information in a related lecture. You are scored on your ability to clearly integrate and relay important points from the passage and the lecture.

The reading passage provides a general definition of a term, process, or idea. The lecture covers the same topic, giving examples or detailed information to illustrate the content from the passage. The question asks that you combine and relay the main points from the passage and lecture.

For this task, you are allowed 40 to 50 seconds to read the 75- to 100-word passage and write down notes for it. The corresponding lecture is 60 to 90 seconds long (150 to 220 words). During this time, a photograph of a speaker appears. A timer bar shows how much time has passed during the lecture.

After listening to the lecture, read and listen to the prompt, which stays on the screen.

Prompt

Using the examples from the lecture, explain how the information in the passage relates to the information presented in the lecture.

You are then given 30 seconds to prepare your response and 60 seconds to speak.

The topics discussed in the passage and the lecture are taken from a range of areas, such as psychology, history, literature, and biology. The task does not require specific knowledge of any subject.

Although you do not need to summarize all the information from the passage and lecture, you do need to provide enough information so that a listener unfamiliar with the passage and lecture would understand your response.

2. NECESSARY SKILLS FOR TASK 4

You must be able to:

- paraphrase subject matter from written and spoken sources
- identify and summarize major point from written and spoken sources
- convey relationships between abstract concepts and concrete information
- connect a spoken example to a written term, process, or concept

HACKING STRATEGY

STEP 1. OUTLINE YOUR RESPONSE

- Take notes as you read the passage
- Take notes as you listen to the lecture
- Read the prompt carefully

STEP 2. PREPARE YOUR RESPONSE

- Summarize the passage and lecture information
- Make sure that you can fully address the prompt

STEP 3. DELIVER YOUR RESPONSE

- Respond with coherent sentences
- Add transition words between ideas

HACKING STRATEGY EXAMPLE

STEP 1. OUTLINE YOUR RESPONSE

Take notes on important information as you read the passage and listen to the corresponding lecture. Do not take notes using full sentences, as you will not have the time to do so.

PASSAGE

Classicism in Renaissance Paintings

From the 14th to the 17th centuries, many artists in Europe began rejecting the rigid beliefs of their time. The era has been called the *Renaissance*, or "rebirth," because during this time, people were inspired to revive the ideals and artistic accomplishments of ancient cultures. Artists began thinking of ancient Greco-Roman creations as models, or "classics."

Classicism was the resulting art trend. It emphasized symmetry, which was important to the ancient cultures, as can be seen in Greek temples and Roman bridges. Classicist painters during the Renaissance planned their paintings carefully. Images of people and objects are balanced, often within symmetrical shapes, so scenes appear to be calm and orderly.

LECTURE

Now let's turn our focus to Raphael, an Italian artist who's strongly associated with Renaissance Classicism. Let's discuss one of Raphael's paintings called The School of Athens.

The School of Athens *depicts dozens of ancient philosophers and mathematicians, most of them Greek. They're talking to and learning from each other even though, in real life, they lived at different times. Clearly, Raphael was celebrating the thinkers. At the same time, he was indicating how much he admired the Greco-Roman emphasis on debate and education.*

The men in the picture are all gathered on the steps of a temple that's open to blue skies. The figures seem to be placed randomly, but on closer inspection, they stand within triangular and circular patterns, measured and balanced within the frame. Thus, as in ancient Greek art, there's an underlying feeling of order and perfection to the painting.

PASSAGE NOTES

Main Idea: *Ren. = 14-17 c. art insp. by Greece & Rome*

- Details: *Ren. = "rebirth"; learning → classics = models*
  Classicism = Ren. art trend → symmetry and "order"

LECTURE NOTES

Topic: *Raphael, Ren. ideals in School of Athens*

Example 1: *ancient Greek phils. in painting*

- Details: *good of debate, edu.*

Example 2: *set on steps of Greek temple*

- Details: *triangles, circles, balanced = order*

Prompt

Using the example from the lecture and information from the reading, explain how Raphael's *The School of Athens* embodies many Renaissance values and ideals.

STEP 2. Prepare Your Response

During the 30-second preparation time, make sure that your notes address all the points in the prompt, and use the information in your notes to organize your response. Because you have so little time to prepare your response, do not write complete sentences.

1) Make sure that you can summarize the main idea of the passage.
   From Notes → Main Idea: *Renaissance = 14th-17th-century art inspired by Greece & Rome*

2) Make sure that you can explain the main topic of the lecture.
   From Notes → Topic: *Raphael, Renaissance ideals in* The School of Athens
   Example 1: *ancient Greek philosophies in painting*
   Example 2: *set on steps of Greek temple*

3) Explain how The School of Athens embodies Renaissance values and ideals.
   From Notes → Details: *(P) Renaissance ideals = learning, order, Greek/Rome*
   (L) painting = philosophies → good of debate, education
   painting = triangles, circles, balanced = order

STEP 3. Deliver Your Response

Use the outline that you created in STEP 2 to guide you as you deliver your response. Respond using complete sentences, and add transition words to show how ideas relate to one another.

Classicism refers to an art trend that developed during the European Renaissance. The School of Athens, *a painting by Raphael, highlights many features of the Classicist style. The painting shows a number of ancient Greek philosophers talking to one another on the steps of a Greek temple. Even though the people actually lived at different times, in the painting they are conversing with each other.* ***Thus,*** *Raphael was showing how much he valued the "classic" Greek method of learning through debate and critical thinking.* ***Therefore,*** *as The School of Athens demonstrates, Classicism's subject matter supports ancient Greco-Roman values.*

In terms of technique, Classicism adopted the Greek and Roman ideals of symmetry and balance. ***For example,*** *in* The School of Athens, *Raphael seems to place the men in natural groups, but actually they're situated within symmetrical circles and triangles. The painting achieves a feeling of orderliness, which was an artistic goal for ancient Greeks and Romans.*

STEP 1A. OUTLINE YOUR RESPONSE

NOTE-TAKING STRATEGIES

Taking notes quickly during the reading and listening portions of this task is crucial, as you can use your notes to help outline your speaking response. When taking notes, you should be able to **abbreviate**, or shorten, common words or phrases and **condense information** in order to save time.

Tips for taking notes

- Only write down key points/information that you will use in your response.
- Because of time constraints, do not write using full sentences.
- Make sure that you can understand your own abbreviations.

TAKING NOTES ON THE PASSAGE

The passage will discuss an academic topic. Therefore, successful notes will state the topic and list any definitions or details that relate to the topic.

PASSAGE

Perpetual Meadows

Sometimes in nature, a grassy meadow is a relatively temporary habitat, such as a place where trees have burned but not yet grown back. However, some meadows are permanent, or *perpetual meadows*. In these, one or more constant environmental factors discourage the growth of shrubs and trees yet favor the growth of grasses and flowers.

PASSAGE NOTES

Main Idea: *perpetual/permanent grass habitat*

- **Details:** *env. factors create ↓ trees, ↑ grasses*

Read the passage, and fill out the note template that follows.

PASSAGE

Plant Defensive Chemistry

Because plants cannot move around like animals can, they have developed countless ways of protecting themselves. One basic method is chemical defense. For example, a plant might produce chemicals that deter predators. The chemicals might make the plant's leaves and stems toxic to insects or unappetizing to animals.

Although it is very difficult to prove, ecologists also suspect that some plants engage in *allelopathy*. That is, a plant targets other plants indirectly by releasing chemicals into the soil, negatively affecting microbes and nutrients there so that other plants cannot thrive. Suppressing other plants would give a plant more access to nutrients and sunshine for itself.

PASSAGE NOTES

Main Idea: ____________________

- Details: ____________________

____

____

STEP 1B. OUTLINE YOUR RESPONSE

TAKING NOTES ON THE LECTURE

The lecture presents a topic that relates to or elaborates upon the information in the passage. In your notes, identify the lecture topic and its relationship to the information in the passage.

LECTURE

Okay, let's take a look at a specific type of perpetual meadow called an alpine meadow. Alpine meadows occur at high altitudes — that is, high up on mountains. You can imagine the cold conditions at these high altitudes. What would happen if a tree started to grow in such intense cold? Well, the tree's sap, which is the liquid within its trunk, would freeze, and the tree's roots would have a difficult time spreading in the frozen soil.

Grasses are quite different and can easily adapt to the cold conditions. Grasses have roots that can spread in a small amount of soil and survive under the winter snowpack. Within a very short warm season, grasses can sprout, flower, and produce seeds.

LECTURE NOTES

Topic: *high alt. → env. for alpine/perpetual meadow*

Example 1: *trees @ high alt.*

- **Details:** *cold freezes sap, stops tree roots*

Example 2: *grasses @ high alt.*

- **Details:** *roots survive cold ↓ground, sprout in short season*

The following lecture corresponds with the passage from the previous page. Read the lecture, and fill out the note template that follows.

LECTURE

The Lamiaceae family of plants includes 6,000 species from around the world. Sometimes called the "mint family," it includes not only peppermint but also many herbs that you probably use yourselves in cooking, such as oregano, thyme, basil, and sage.

Plants in the Lamiaceae family tend to have a strong odor that comes from oils produced on the plants' leaves and stems. The odor may serve as a chemical defense. Deer appear to dislike the odor and refrain from eating many species in the mint family. In addition, the oils in some of these plants repel insects. Some can even be used as mosquito repellent.

The strong-smelling oils associated with Lamiaceae may also serve as allelopaths. In other words, plants in the mint family may be able to chemically discourage other plants from growing near them. For example, henbit, a member of the mint family that's considered a weed in North America, may thrive so well in your lawn partly because it chemically inhibits growth of other plants.

LECTURE NOTES

Topic: ______________________________

Example 1: ______________________________

- Details: ______________________________

____

Example 2: ______________________________

- Details: ______________________________

____

STEP 2. PREPARE YOUR RESPONSE

PASSAGE

Perpetual Meadows

Sometimes in nature, a grassy meadow is a relatively temporary habitat, such as a place where trees have burned but not yet grown back. However, some meadows are permanent, or *perpetual meadows*. In these, one or more constant environmental factors discourage the growth of shrubs and trees yet favor the growth of grasses and flowers.

LECTURE

Okay, let's take a look at a specific type of perpetual meadow called an alpine meadow. Alpine meadows occur at high altitudes — that is, high up on mountains. You can imagine the cold conditions at these high altitudes. What would happen if a tree started to grow in such intense cold? Well, the tree's sap, which is the liquid within its trunk, would freeze, and the tree's roots would have a difficult time spreading in the frozen soil.

Grasses are quite different and can easily adapt to the cold conditions. Grasses have roots that can spread in a small amount of soil and survive under the winter snowpack. Within a very short warm season, grasses can sprout, flower, and produce seeds.

PASSAGE NOTES

Topic: *perpetual/permanent grass habitat*

- Details: *env. factors create ↓ trees, ↑ grasses*

LECTURE NOTES

Topic: *high alt. → env. for alpine/perpetual meadow*

Example 1: *trees @ high alt.*

- Details: *cold freezes sap, stops tree roots*

Example 2: *grasses @ high alt.*

- Details: *roots survive cold ↓ground,*
  sprout in short season

Once you have finished listening to the lecture, the prompt will appear on the screen.

Prompt

Using the example of alpine meadows, explain how environmental conditions create perpetual meadows.

After reading the prompt, you have 30 seconds to prepare your response. During your preparation time, organize your notes so you can address the following pieces of information in your response.

1) Make sure that you can summarize the main idea of the passage.

From Notes → Main Idea: *perpetual/permanent grass habitat*

2) Make sure you can describe the main topic of the lecture.

From Notes → Topic: *high altitude → environment for alpine/perpetual meadow*

Example 1: *trees at high altitude*

Example 2: *grasses at high altitude*

3) Make sure that you can explain how environmental conditions create "perpetual meadows."

From Notes → Details: *(P) environment factors create less trees, more grasses*

(L) trees → cold freezes sap, stops tree roots

grasses → roots survive cold underground, sprout in short season

Read the passage and the lecture. Then prepare a Task 4 response, using the template below. Review your notes from the previous practices if necessary.

PASSAGE

Plant Defensive Chemistry

Because plants cannot move around like animals can, they have developed countless ways of protecting themselves. One basic method is chemical defense. For example, a plant might produce chemicals that deter predators. The chemicals might make the plant's leaves and stems toxic to insects or unappetizing to animals.

Although it is very difficult to prove, ecologists also suspect that some plants engage in *allelopathy*. That is, a plant targets other plants indirectly by releasing chemicals into the soil, negatively affecting microbes and nutrients there so that other plants cannot thrive. Suppressing other plants would give a plant more access to nutrients and sunshine for itself.

LECTURE

The Lamiaceae family of plants includes 6,000 species from around the world. Sometimes called the "mint family," it includes not only peppermint but also many herbs that you probably use yourselves in cooking, such as oregano, thyme, basil, and sage.

Plants in the Lamiaceae family tend to have a strong odor that comes from oils produced on the plants' leaves and stems. The odor may serve as a chemical defense. Deer appear to dislike the odor and refrain from eating many species in the mint family. In addition, the oils in some of these plants repel insects. Some can even be used as mosquito repellent.

The strong-smelling oils associated with Lamiaceae may also serve as allelopaths. In other words, plants in the mint family may be able to chemically discourage other plants from growing near them. For example, henbit, a member of the mint family that's considered a weed in North America, may thrive so well in your lawn partly because it chemically inhibits growth of other plants.

Prompt

Using the information from the passage and the example from the lecture, explain some of the ways that plants defend themselves from animals and other plants.

1) Summarize the main idea of the passage.

From Notes → Main Idea: ______________________________

2) Summarize the lecture information.

From Notes → Topic: ______________________________

Example 1: ______________________________

Example 2: ______________________________

3) Explain how plants defend themselves from animals and other plants.

From Notes → Details: ______________________________

____

STEP 3. DELIVER YOUR RESPONSE

Use the outline that you created in STEP 2 to guide you as you respond to the prompt.

Prompt

Using the example of alpine meadows, explain how environmental conditions create perpetual meadows.

- **Reading Summary:** The first sentence of your response should be a summary of the information in the passage.
- **Lecture Topic:** Then describe the examples discussed in the lecture.
- **Passage/Lecture Relationship:** Lastly, connect the passage information to the lecture's example(s), being sure to fully respond to the prompt.
- Include **transition words** in your response to clarify the relationships between related ideas.

Example Response

	Notes	Response
Passage Summary	*perpetual/permanent grass habitat*	*A perpetual meadow is a field that's maintained by some fairly permanent natural condition.*
Lecture Main Idea	*high alt. → env. for alpine/ perpetual meadow*	***For example**, the lecture talks about how cold temperatures maintain alpine meadows high in the mountains.*
Passage/ Lecture Relationship	*env. factors create ↓ trees, ↑ grasses* *trees → cold (alpine) freezes sap, stops tree roots* *grasses → roots survive ↓ground, ↑ in short season*	*Extreme cold keeps trees from invading the area because tree sap freezes and tree roots can't grow in frozen soil.* ***At the same time**, grass roots can survive underground throughout long, snowy winters, and then in even a short summer, grasses can sprout and produce seeds quickly.*

Review the following passage, lecture, and prompt. Then write a Task 4 response. Review your notes from the previous practices if necessary. Once you have written down your response, **say it aloud to yourself, a friend, a classmate, or a family member**.

PASSAGE

Plant Defensive Chemistry

Because plants cannot move around like animals can, they have developed countless ways of protecting themselves. One basic method is chemical defense. For example, a plant might produce chemicals that deter predators. The chemicals might make the plant's leaves and stems toxic to insects or unappetizing to animals.

Although it is very difficult to prove, ecologists also suspect that some plants engage in *allelopathy*. That is, a plant targets other plants indirectly by releasing chemicals into the soil, negatively affecting microbes and nutrients there so that other plants cannot thrive. Suppressing other plants would give a plant more access to nutrients and sunshine for itself.

LECTURE

The Lamiaceae family of plants includes 6,000 species from around the world. Sometimes called the "mint family," it includes not only peppermint but also many herbs that you probably use yourselves in cooking, such as oregano, thyme, basil, and sage.

Plants in the Lamiaceae family tend to have a strong odor that comes from oils produced on the plants' leaves and stems. The odor may serve as a chemical defense. Deer appear to dislike the odor and refrain from eating many species in the mint family. In addition, the oils in some of these plants repel insects. Some can even be used as mosquito repellent.

The strong-smelling oils associated with Lamiaceae may also serve as allelopaths. In other words, plants in the mint family may be able to chemically discourage other plants from growing near them. For example, henbit, a member of the mint family that's considered a weed in North America, may thrive so well in your lawn partly because it chemically inhibits growth of other plants.

Prompt

Using the information from the passage and the example from the lecture, explain some of the ways that plants defend themselves from animals and other plants.

Response

EXERCISE 1

Following the steps below, develop a response to the following prompt.

STEP 1. OUTLINE YOUR RESPONSE

PASSAGE

Types of Body Language

When our movements or facial expressions communicate our thoughts or feelings, we are using *body language*. Sociologists use the term *involuntary body language* for signals that we do not necessarily realize we are conveying. Such unconscious gestures tend to be the same among all cultures. On the other hand, *voluntary body language* describes people's intentional use of body language, such as a wave. Intentional signals are usually cultural gestures that have to be learned.

LECTURE

A great way to illustrate the differences between voluntary and involuntary body language is to describe gestures involved in greeting. Imagine two acquaintances, a man and a woman, happen to meet at a store. Even before they speak, their body language communicates greetings.

We can expect that there would first be involuntary body language. For example, when the people first see each other, one may flash her eyebrows up and down. This is a signal that she recognizes the other person. But that other person may draw his eyebrows together in the middle. This may indicate that he's confused or is trying to remember the other person's name. Probably neither person is consciously aware of sending or receiving the quick signals.

Next, the two people may intentionally and voluntarily engage in a polite greeting gesture. Depending on their culture, they may wave, reach out to shake hands, lean forward to kiss each other on both cheeks, or stop and bow. All of these gestures indicate good intent toward the other. So even without words, the two acquaintances communicate a great deal within a few seconds.

PASSAGE NOTES

Main Idea: ______________________

____

- Details: ______________________

____

LECTURE NOTES

Topic: ______________________

Example 1: ______________________

- Details: ______________________

Example 2: ______________________

- Details: ______________________

Prompt

Using information from the reading and the lecture, explain how people use voluntary and involuntary body language when interacting with each other.

STEP 2. PREPARE YOUR RESPONSE

00:00:30

1) Summarize the main idea of the passage.

From Notes → Main Idea: ______________________________

2) Summarize the lecture information.

From Notes → Topic: ______________________________

Example 1: ______________________________

Example 2: ______________________________

3) Explain how the lecture information relates to the passage.

From Notes → Details: ______________________________

____

STEP 3. DELIVER YOUR RESPONSE

00:01:00

Response

____

____

____

____

____

____

____

Now practice saying your response aloud. If possible, have a friend/classmate fill out this checklist as you say your response to him or her. If you are by yourself, record and listen to your response, and then fill out the checklist below on your own.

Deliver your response within 60 seconds.

Task 4 Response Checklist

	Yes	Somewhat	No
• Does the speaker accurately summarize the concept discussed in the reading passage?			
• Does the speaker accurately summarize the example(s) presented in the lecture?			
• Does the speaker explain how the example(s) in the lecture relate to the concept described in the passage?			
• Does the speaker deliver an organized response by using transition words and proper sentence structures?			
• Does the speaker deliver a coherent response by using appropriate tone and pronunciation?			
• Does the speaker finish within the time limit?		X	

PASSAGE NOTES

Main Idea: *body lang. = movement/face → thoughts/feelings*

- **Details:** *involun. body lang. = don't realize*
  volun. body lang. = intentional, cultural

LECTURE NOTES

Topic: *body lang. & gestures of greeting*

Example 1: *involun. body lang.*

- **Details:** *brows ↑ & ↓=recognize, brows together=confused*

Example 2: *volun. body lang.*

- **Details:** *cultural greeting (wave, bow), good intent*

1) Summarize the main idea of the passage.

From Notes → Main Idea: *body language. = movement/face → thoughts/feelings*

2) Summarize the lecture information.

From Notes → Topic: *gestures of greeting*

Example 1: *involuntary body language*

Example 2: *voluntary body language*

3) Explain how the lecture information relates to the passage.

From Notes → Details: *involuntary = eyebrow movement → recognize/not recognize person*
voluntary = cultural greetings → wave, bow; good intent

Response

The reading passage talks about body language, which describes non-vocal ways of communicating. Body language can be involuntary, meaning that a person doesn't realize that they're communicating anything, or voluntary, meaning that a person is intentionally using body language. The lecture gives examples of both kinds of body language by talking about how people use body language when they greet each other. First, when two people see each other, they might move their eyebrows to show either recognition of or unfamiliarity with the other person. These eyebrow movements are examples of involuntary body language. However, when the people get closer, they might use voluntary body language, such as a wave or a bow, as a way of saying "hello."

EXERCISE 2

Following the steps below, develop a response to the following prompt.

STEP 1. OUTLINE YOUR RESPONSE

PASSAGE

Circadian Rhythms

Circadian rhythms in living organisms are patterns of activity — such as regular periods of alertness and inactivity — over a 24-hour period. One function of circadian rhythms is to ensure that organisms are active when food sources are accessible. In animals, the rhythms also produce a sleepy feeling when it is safest for the animal to sleep. In other words, circadian rhythms create a natural routine that helps an organism thrive in its environment.

LECTURE

You've been reading about circadian rhythms, the daily routines of living creatures, and how such rhythms help creatures adapt to habitats.

For instance, consider a group of rabbits adapting gradually to a hot desert. The single most important adaptation for these rabbits would be to become nocturnal. Rabbits require a great deal of plant food, so they'd need many hours to forage in desert areas for sufficient food. Foraging all day in the desert would make them very tired and thirsty. However, hopping around in the cool of the night would be an efficient way to avoid heat exhaustion and dehydration.

Furthermore, it's safer for desert rabbits to sleep during the day because their daytime predators are hawks and eagles, birds that rely on eyesight. During the day, rabbits need to keep out of sight and stay still, so it's a great time to sleep. Daytime is also when their nocturnal predators, such as cats and foxes, are sleeping. Those cats and foxes will be awake and relying on their senses of smell and hearing at night, so hiding will be impossible. Rabbits need to be alert and able to run from them at night.

PASSAGE NOTES

Main Idea: ____________________

____

- Details: ____________________

____

LECTURE NOTES

Topic: ____________________

Example 1: ____________________

- Details: ____________________

Example 2: ____________________

- Details: ____________________

Prompt

Using examples and details from the lecture, explain how circadian rhythms help animals adapt to their environments.

STEP 2. PREPARE YOUR RESPONSE

00:00:30

1) Summarize the main idea of the passage.

   From Notes → Main Idea: ______________________________

2) Summarize the lecture information.

   From Notes → Topic: ______________________________

   Example 1: ______________________________

   Example 2: ______________________________

3) Explain how the lecture information relates to the passage.

   From Notes → Details: ______________________________

   ____

STEP 3. DELIVER YOUR RESPONSE

00:01:00

Response

____

____

____

____

____

____

____

Now practice saying your response aloud. If possible, have a friend/classmate fill out this checklist as you say your response to him or her. If you are by yourself, record and listen to your response, and then fill out the checklist below on your own.

Deliver your response within 60 seconds.

Task 4 Response Checklist

	Yes	Somewhat	No
• Does the speaker accurately summarize the concept discussed in the reading passage?			
• Does the speaker accurately summarize the example(s) presented in the lecture?			
• Does the speaker explain how the example(s) in the lecture relate to the concept described in the passage?			
• Does the speaker deliver an organized response by using transition words and proper sentence structures?			
• Does the speaker deliver a coherent response by using appropriate tone and pronunciation?			
• Does the speaker finish within the time limit?		╳	

PASSAGE NOTES

Main Idea: *circadian rhythms = 24-hr. wake/rest cycle*

- **Details:** *active when food / sleepy when safe natural routine for an env.*

LECTURE NOTES

Topic: *rabbit → nocturnal in desert env.*

Example 1: *find food @ night*

- **Details:** *avoid overheating*

Example 2: *sleep during day*

- **Details:** *hide from bird predators, alert for night predators*

1) Summarize the main idea of the passage.

From Notes → Main Idea: *circadian rhythms = 24-hour wake/rest cycle*

2) Summarize the lecture information.

From Notes → Topic: *rabbit → nocturnal in desert environment*

Example 1: *find food at night*

Example 2: *sleep during day*

3) Explain how the lecture information relates to the passage.

From Notes → Details: *find food at night → avoid overheating*

sleep during day → hide from bird, alert for night predators

Response

The reading passage describes circadian rhythms, which are 24-hour cycles that help an animal survive by making an animal feel active when food's available and sleepy when it's safest to rest. The lecture elaborates on this topic by talking about rabbits that have to become nocturnal to survive in a desert environment. For example, the desert rabbits are better off searching for food all night than all day under the hot Sun; being nocturnal keeps from overheating. The lecture also says that it's safest for rabbits to sleep during the day, when their eyesight-dependent bird predators are watching. It allows them to be ready to run from nocturnal predators, which also sleep during the day.

EXERCISE 3

Following the steps below, develop a response to the following prompt.

STEP 1. OUTLINE YOUR RESPONSE

PASSAGE

Impressionism

Impressionism is a 19th-century painting technique that aims to capture a quick "impression" of an everyday scene. Impressionist painters rejected the traditional artistic goal of creating an exact representation of a subject. Rather, they wanted to reveal all that the human eye takes in with a quick glance, including the tiny movements of light and shadow. Thus, one Impressionist technique is the use of color to give the appearance of reflected light. Another technique is the use of quick brush strokes that look unblended but nevertheless present an unmistakable image.

LECTURE

Let's look at the painting called Impression, Sunrise, *by Claude Monet. In 1872, when it was first shown, this painting was ridiculed as being unfinished. The subject is a simple sunrise at an industrial harbor, with a couple of figures in a small rowboat in the foreground. Of course, today the painting is revered; it is considered a brilliant example of Impressionism for a couple of reasons.*

First, Monet's use of color suggests misty sunrise, with gray, white, and yellow streaks. The sun is an orb reflected in the water by diagonal orange lines, and in the sky with a yellow-orange mist. The boat and figures in the foreground are simply dark smudges, blending into the shadows they cast, like a brief interruption of the massive reflection. Even tiny movements in the water are suggested by the dark blue lines of waves' shadows.

Also, the painting conveys a feeling that everything in it is moving: clouds, sun, water, boats. Monet achieved this effect by quickly applying short brushstrokes to the canvas. Up close, the painting looks like a child's clumsy effort. But when you step back and look at it with a kind of "soft focus," you have a sudden feeling of recognition. Even if you have never been to that place, you sense something familiar about a cold, misty morning.

PASSAGE NOTES

Main Idea: ______________________________

____

- Details: ______________________________

____

LECTURE NOTES

Topic: ______________________________

Example 1: ______________________________

- Details: ______________________________

Example 2: ______________________________

- Details: ______________________________

Prompt

The professor discusses an example of an impressionist painting. Describe Impressionism and explain how the painting discussed embodies impressionist style.

STEP 2. PREPARE YOUR RESPONSE

00:00:30

1) Summarize the main idea of the passage.

From Notes → Main Idea: ______________________________

2) Summarize the lecture information.

From Notes → Topic: ______________________________

Example 1: ______________________________

Example 2: ______________________________

3) Explain how the lecture information relates to the passage.

From Notes → Details: ______________________________

____

STEP 3. DELIVER YOUR RESPONSE

00:01:00

Response

____

____

____

____

____

____

____

Now practice saying your response aloud. If possible, have a friend/classmate fill out this checklist as you say your response to him or her. If you are by yourself, record and listen to your response, and then fill out the checklist below on your own.

Deliver your response within 60 seconds.

Task 4 Response Checklist

	Yes	Somewhat	No
• Does the speaker accurately summarize the concept discussed in the reading passage?			
• Does the speaker accurately summarize the example(s) presented in the lecture?			
• Does the speaker explain how the example(s) in the lecture relate to the concept described in the passage?			
• Does the speaker deliver an organized response by using transition words and proper sentence structures?			
• Does the speaker deliver a coherent response by using appropriate tone and pronunciation?			
• Does the speaker finish within the time limit?		X	

PASSAGE NOTES

Main Idea: *Impressionism = quick glance, light, shadow, not exact outline*

- **Details:** *two techniques*

1 → color, reflection of light;

2 → quick brush strokes, but clear image

LECTURE NOTES

Topic: Impression, Sunrise, *Monet, ex. of Impr.*

Example 1: *color → reflected light, shadow*

- **Details:** *colorful = sunrise, shadows "interrupt"*

Example 2: *brushstrokes = movement*

- **Details:** *up close → unclear, far away → clear*

1) Summarize the main idea of the passage.

From Notes → Main Idea: *Impressionism = painting first impressions of nature*

2) Summarize the lecture information.

From Notes → Topic: *Monet's* Impression, Sunrise

Example 1: *color conveys reflected light and shadow*

Example 2: *brushstrokes create movement*

3) Explain how the lecture information relates to the passage.

From Notes → Details: *bright colors create sunrise, interrupted by shadows*

quick brushstrokes make image unclear up close but clear far away

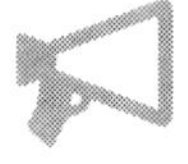

Response

The reading passage discusses the painting style called Impressionism, which gives a momentary "impression" of a scene rather than a perfect outline. Impressionist artists try to depict light and movement through their color choices and brushstrokes. The lecture elaborates upon the reading by describing features of Monet's painting Impression, Sunrise. First, light colors such as gray, white, and yellow illuminate the sky and water, and these colors are contrasted by a few dark-colored shapes such as shadows from waves and small boats. Second, the quick brush strokes don't look sophisticated close up, but the scene appears realistic from farther back.

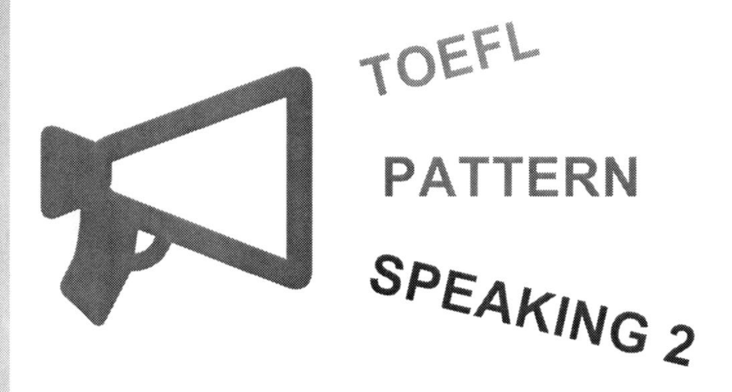

Task 5

CHAPTER 5

Campus Situation

(Listening)

Campus Situation

GENERAL BACKGROUND INFORMATION

1. EXPLANATION OF TASK 5

Task 5 requires that you listen to a short conversation that one might hear in a university setting. The conversation will be between a student and another student, a professor, or a university employee.

Some common conversation topics include:

- academic problems (e.g. bad grades, difficulty deciding on a major)
- scheduling conflicts or absences
- financial difficulties

In the conversation, a student will state an issue or difficulty he or she is having, and the other speaker will provide two possible solutions.

After listening to the conversation, you will be given a prompt related to what you have heard. The prompt appears on your computer screen and is read aloud by a narrator.

Prompt

Briefly summarize the student's issue. Then state which of the proposed solutions you prefer.
If you have a different solution, include it in your response. Explain your decision.

When providing a preferred solution in your response, you can either use one of the solutions from the conversation or come up with your own solution. Similarly, when producing reasons to support your preferred solution, you can either use the reasons stated in the conversation or create your own.

After the question is presented, you have 20 seconds to prepare your response. At the end, you will hear a short beep. The clock then changes to "Response Time" and begins to count down.

You have 60 seconds to respond. At the end of the 60 seconds, the recording ends and a new message alerts you that the response time is over.

You may take notes while listening to the conversation and during your preparation time. You also may check your notes when responding to the question.

2. NECESSARY SKILLS FOR TASK 5

You must be able to:

- understand information from spoken sources regarding campus-based subject matter
- identify and summarize major points and important details from spoken sources
- discuss the connection between issues and their proposed solutions

HACKING STRATEGY

STEP 1. OUTLINE YOUR RESPONSE

- Take notes as you listen to the conversation
- Read the prompt carefully

STEP 2. PREPARE YOUR RESPONSE

- Explain the student's problem
- State which solution you prefer and why you prefer it

STEP 3. DELIVER YOUR RESPONSE

- Respond with coherent sentences
- Add transition words between ideas

HACKING STRATEGY EXAMPLE

STEP 1. OUTLINE YOUR RESPONSE

Take notes on important information as you listen to the conversation. Do not take notes using full sentences, as you will not have time to do so.

CONVERSATION

F: *What's wrong, Carl?*

M: *Oh, I'm failing my calculus class again.*

F: *I'm sorry to hear that. But you know, I think I can help you.*

M: *Really? How so?*

F: *Well, I'm good at math, so I could tutor you if you want.*

M: *Thanks, Judy. That's sweet of you.*

F: *Another possibility is to drop the class and take Professor Dodd's class next semester. His class is easier than the one you're taking right now. You might find that it works better for you.*

F: Female Student / **M:** Male Student

CONVERSATION NOTES

Problem: *man failing calc.*

- **Solution 1:** *woman can tutor him*
- **Solution 2:** *drop the class & take it next semester*

After taking notes, carefully read the prompt, making sure that you know exactly what it asks you to do.

Prompt

Briefly summarize the problem that the speakers discuss. Then state which of the two solutions from the conversation you would recommend. Explain the reasons for your recommendation.

STEP 2. Prepare Your Response

00:00:20

During the 20-second preparation time, make sure that your notes address all the points in the prompt, and use the information in your notes to organize your response. Because you have so little time to prepare your response, do not write complete sentences.

1) Make sure that you can summarize the student's problem.
   From Notes → Problem: *man failing calculus*

2) Make sure that you can identify which of the two proposed solutions you prefer.
   Preferred solution: *drop the class and take it next semester*

3) Make sure that you can give two reasons explaining why you prefer this solution.
   Reason 1 : *class easier, instructor clearer*
   Reason 2: *even with tutoring, still difficult*

STEP 3. Deliver Your Response

00:01:00

Use the outline that you created in STEP 2 to guide you as you deliver your response. Respond using complete sentences, and add transition words to show how ideas relate to one another.

The man's failing his calculus class again. The woman suggests that she either tutor him, or that he drop the class and take an easier calculus class next semester. Personally, I think the man should take the easier class next semester. ***One reason*** *is that doing so will allow him to start fresh with a new instructor. The class offered next semester is less difficult, and the professor might provide clearer instruction to aid the student's understanding of the subject.* ***Another reason*** *to take the class next semester is to avoid falling behind in his class this semester. Even with tutoring for his current class, he might continue to have difficulty.*

STEP 1. OUTLINE YOUR RESPONSE

NOTE-TAKING STRATEGIES

Taking notes quickly during the reading and listening portions of this task is crucial, as you can use your notes to help outline your speaking response. When taking notes, you should be able to **abbreviate**, or shorten, common words or phrases and **condense information** in order to save time.

Tips for taking notes

- Only write down key points/information that you will use in your response.
- Because of time constraints, do not write using full sentences.
- Make sure that you can understand your own abbreviations.

TAKING NOTES ON THE CONVERSATION

When taking notes, be sure to identify the **problem** and whom it affects. Then write down the **two solutions** proposed and mark which solution you think will be more effective.

CONVERSATION

F: *What's wrong, Brad?*
M: *Ah, it's my car again, Juanita. The engine died.*
F: *Oh, no. So how will you get to school now?*
M: *I don't know. That's why I'm so upset.*
F: *The university's bus-system works well. That's how I got to class last year, and I was never late.*
M: *Thanks, I'll definitely check the bus schedule for this semester.*
F: *Or you could always ride your bike to campus. That way, you could get some exercise while still getting to class on time.*
M: *Yeah, I guess that's true, too. Thanks for the advice!*

F: *Female Student* / **M:** *Male Student*

CONVERSATION NOTES

Problem: *man → car's engine died, no way to get to school*

- **Solution 1:** *use campus bus system*
- **Solution 2:** *ride bike to campus*

Read the conversation, and fill out the note template that follows.

CONVERSATION

M: *Hey Kimberly, how are things going with your roommate?*

F: *Not good, Amir. Even after I talked to her about being noisy and leaving the dorm room a mess, she's still loud and isn't picking up after herself.*

M: *Hmm. Maybe you should try renting your own room off-campus.*

F: *Yeah, maybe. But I like living on campus; it's so convenient.*

M: *Well, you could ask to switch rooms and get a new roommate. I think they'll do that for you.*

F: *I suppose. But what if a new roommate's worse than the one I have now?*

M: *Male Student* / **F:** *Female Student*

CONVERSATION NOTES

Problem: ________________________________

- Solution 1: ________________________________
- Solution 2: ________________________________

STEP 2. PREPARE YOUR RESPONSE

CONVERSATION

F: *What's wrong, Brad?*

M: *Ah, it's my car again, Juanita. The engine died.*

F: *Oh, no. So how will you get to school now?*

M: *I don't know. That's why I'm so upset.*

F: *The university's bus-system works well. That's how I got to class last year, and I was never late.*

M: *Thanks, I'll definitely check the bus schedule for this semester.*

F: *Or you could always ride your bike to campus. That way, you could get some exercise while still getting to class on time.*

M: *Yeah, I guess that's true, too. Thanks for the advice!*

F: *Female Student* / **M:** *Male Student*

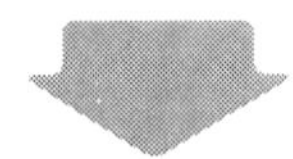

CONVERSATION NOTES

Problem: *man → car's engine died, no way to get to school*

- **Solution 1:** *use campus bus system*
- **Solution 2:** *ride bike to campus*

After taking notes on the conversation, carefully read the prompt that appears on the screen. Make sure that you understand exactly what the prompt is asking you to do.

Prompt

The two students talk about two solutions to the male student's problem. Explain what the male student's problem is. Then state which possible solution you prefer and explain your preference.

After reading the prompt, you have 20 seconds to prepare your response. During your preparation time, organize your notes so you can address the following pieces of information in your response.

1) Make sure that you can summarize the student's problem.

From Notes → Problem: *man → car engine died, no way to get to school*

2) Make sure that you can identify which of the two proposed solutions your prefer.

From Notes → Preferred solution 2: *ride bike to campus*

3) Make sure that you can give two reasons explaining why you prefer this solution.

From Notes → Reason 1: *good exercise, rewarding*

Reason 2: *save $ on bus fare and gas*

Review the following conversation. Then prepare a Task 5 response, using the template below. Review your notes from the previous page if necessary.

CONVERSATION

M: *Hey Kimberly, how are things going with your roommate?*

F: *Not good, Amir. Even after I talked to her about being noisy and leaving the dorm room a mess, she's still loud and isn't picking up after herself.*

M: *Hmm. Maybe you should try renting your own room off-campus.*

F: *Yeah, maybe. But I like living on campus; it's so convenient.*

M: *Well you could ask to switch rooms and get a new roommate. I think they will do that for you.*

F: *I suppose. But what if a new roommate is worse than the one I have now?*

M: *Male Student* / **F:** *Female Student*

Prompt

The students discuss two solutions to the female student's problem. Explain what the student's problem is. Then state which possible solution you prefer and explain your preference.

1) Summarize the student's problem.

   From Notes → Problem: ______________________________

2) Identify which of the two proposed solutions your prefer.

   Preferred solution: ______________________________

3) Give two reasons explaining why you prefer this solution.

   Reason 1: ______________________________

   Reason 2: ______________________________

STEP 3. DELIVER YOUR RESPONSE

Use the outline that you created in STEP 2 to guide you as you respond to the prompt.

Prompt

The two students talk about two solutions to the male student's problem. Explain what the male student's problem is. Then state which possible solution you prefer and explain your preference.

- **Student's Problem:** The first sentence of your response should be a summary of the student's problem.
- **Preferred Solution:** Then state which of the two solutions presented in the lecture you prefer.
- **Reasons for Preference:** Lastly, give two reasons stating why you prefer this solution. You can either use reasons from the conversation or come up with reasons of your own.
- Include **transition words** in your response to clarify the relationships between ideas.

Example Response

	Notes		Response
Student's Problem	*man → car's engine died, no way to get to school*	➡	*The issue presented in the student conversation is that the man's car has died, leaving him with no way to easily get to class on time.*
Preferred Solution	*ride bike to campus*	➡	*Of the two solutions proposed in the conversation, I think he should choose to ride his bike to class each day.*
Reasons for Preference	*good exercise, rewarding* *save $ on bus fare and gas*	➡	***For one**, he should choose to ride his bike to class because it will provide him with a good source of exercise. **Hence**, riding a bike to class will be rewarding because he'll arrive to class on time and get a great workout.* ***Moreover**, riding his bike to class will save the man money. He won't have to pay any bus fares, and he won't have to spend money on gas or repairs for his car.*

Review the following conversation and prompt. Then write a Task 5 response. Review your notes from the previous practices if necessary. Once you have written down your response, **say it aloud to yourself, a friend, a classmate, or a family member**.

CONVERSATION

M: *Hey Kimberly, how are things going with your roommate?*

F: *Not good, Amir. Even after I talked to her about being noisy and leaving the dorm room a mess, she's still loud and isn't picking up after herself.*

M: *Hmm. Maybe you should try renting your own room off-campus.*

F: *Yeah, maybe. But I like living on campus; it's so convenient.*

M: *Well you could ask to switch rooms and get a new roommate. I think they will do that for you.*

F: *I suppose. But what if a new roommate is worse than the one I have now?*

M: *Male Student* / **F:** *Female Student*

Prompt

The two students talk about two solutions to the male student's problem. Explain what the male student's problem is. Then state which possible solution you prefer and explain your preference.

Response

EXERCISE 1

Following the steps below, develop a response to the following prompt.

STEP 1. OUTLINE YOUR RESPONSE

CONVERSATION

F: *I wish I could figure out what to major in. It's almost the end of our freshman year, and I still have no idea what I want to study.*

M: *Don't worry about it too much; you have until the end of your sophomore year to declare a major.*

F: *I know, but my parents are putting a lot of pressure on me to make up my mind.*

M: *Well, maybe you can just complete all of your general education requirements and use those classes as an opportunity to figure out what you want to do. Your parents can't get too mad at you if you're taking required classes.*

F: *I guess that's true, but I don't want to fall behind my classmates. I'll feel really left out if everyone I know is taking major-specific courses while I'm still in all introductory courses.*

M: *Then you should talk to an academic advisor. After all, they're here to help students figure out what area of study they want to pursue.*

F: *Well, I guess they are. I hadn't thought about that.*

F: *Female Student* / **M:** *Male Student*

CONVERSATION NOTES

Problem: ______________________________

- **Solution 1:** ______________________________
- **Solution 2:** ______________________________

Prompt

The two students talk about two solutions to the female student's problem. Explain what the female student's problem is. Then state which possible solution you prefer and explain your decision.

STEP 2. PREPARE YOUR RESPONSE

00:00:20

1) Summarize the student's problem.

   From Notes → Problem: ______________________________

2) Identify which of the two proposed solutions your prefer.

   Preferred solution: ______________________________

3) Give two reasons explaining why you prefer this solution.

   Reason 1: ______________________________

   Reason 2: ______________________________

STEP 3. DELIVER YOUR RESPONSE

00:01:00

Response

Now practice saying your response aloud. If possible, have a friend/classmate fill out this checklist as you say your response to him or her. If you are by yourself, record and listen to your response, and then fill out the checklist below on your own.

Deliver your response within 60 seconds.

Task 5 Response Checklist

	Yes	Somewhat	No
• Does the speaker explain the problem discussed in the conversation?			
• Does the speaker state which of the two proposed solutions he or she prefers?			
• Does the speaker explain why he or she selected this preferred solution?			
• Does the speaker deliver an organized response by using transition words and proper sentence structures?			
• Does the speaker deliver a coherent response by using appropriate tone and pronunciation?			
• Does the speaker finish within the time limit?		X	

CONVERSATION NOTES

Problem: *woman can't decide on major*

- **Solution 1:** *finish GEs, decide after*
- **Solution 2:** *talk to acad. advisor*

1) Summarize the student's problem.

   From Notes → Problem: *woman can't decide on major*

2) Identify which of the two proposed solutions your prefer.

   Preferred solution: *sol. 1*

3) Give two reasons explaining why you prefer this solution.

   Reason 1: *must finish required classes eventually*

   Reason 2: *chances to determine interests*

Response

The issue in the conversation is that the woman can't decide on a college major, and her parents are pressuring her to make a decision. Of the two solutions the man proposes, I think the woman should complete her general education classes and decide on a major afterward. First, I think this plan is preferable because she'll have to finish her general education classes eventually, so it's probably in her best interest to get them out of the way early in her college career. That way, she won't have to worry about them once she has decided on a major. Second, as the man says, taking a variety of general education classes will give the woman a chance to discover what she's truly interested in.

EXERCISE 2

Following the steps below, develop a response to the following prompt.

STEP 1. OUTLINE YOUR RESPONSE

CONVERSATION

F: *Hey Brad, you look pretty tired. You okay?*

M: *I'm exhausted. I haven't been getting much sleep because the people in the dorm above mine are yelling and stomping around their room until 3 am. It's like I'm living below a family of giants.*

F: *That's unacceptable. You really need to go up there and talk to them about it. Maybe they don't realize how rude they're being.*

M: *Oh, I think they know. Some other people in the dorms have already asked them to be quiet, but they don't really seem to care very much.*

F: *Well, I still think it's worth trying to talk to them face to face.*

M: *Maybe I'll give it a try.*

F: *Or you could always report them to a resident assistant or the campus security.*

M: *Doesn't that seem a little extreme?*

F: *Well, maybe. But if they don't even have the courtesy to keep quiet at 3 am, then I think it might take extreme measures to get them to quiet down.*

F: *Female Student* / **M:** *Male Student*

CONVERSATION NOTES

Problem: ______________________________

- **Solution 1:** ______________________________
- **Solution 2:** ______________________________

Prompt

The two students talk about two solutions to the male student's problem. Explain what the male student's problem is. Then state which possible solution you prefer and explain your preference.

STEP 2. PREPARE YOUR RESPONSE

00:00:20

1) Summarize the student's problem.

   From Notes → Problem: ____________________

2) Identify which of the two proposed solutions your prefer.

   Preferred solution: ____________________

3) Give two reasons explaining why you prefer this solution.

   Reason 1: ____________________

   Reason 2: ____________________

STEP 3. DELIVER YOUR RESPONSE

00:01:00

Response

Now practice saying your response aloud. If possible, have a friend/classmate fill out this checklist as you say your response to him or her. If you are by yourself, record and listen to your response, and then fill out the checklist below on your own.

Deliver your response within 60 seconds.

Task 5 Response Checklist

	Yes	Somewhat	No
• Does the speaker explain the problem discussed in the conversation?			
• Does the speaker state which of the two proposed solutions he or she prefers?			
• Does the speaker explain why he or she selected this preferred solution?			
• Does the speaker deliver an organized response by using transition words and proper sentence structures?			
• Does the speaker deliver a coherent response by using appropriate tone and pronunciation?			
• Does the speaker finish within the time limit?		X	

CONVERSATION NOTES

Problem: *man has noisy neighbors*

- **Solution 1:** *talk to them in person*
- **Solution 2:** *report them to RA or security*

1) Summarize the student's problem.

   From Notes → Problem: *man has noisy neighbors*

2) Identify which of the two proposed solutions your prefer.

   Preferred solution: *sol. 2*

3) Give two reasons explaining why you prefer this solution.

   Reason 1: *they've already been asked nicely*

   Reason 2: *man will remain anonymous*

Response

The man in the conversation claims that he has very noisy neighbors who live in the dorm room above his. The woman encourages him either to speak his noisy neighbors about the disturbances, or to talk to a resident assistant or campus security. Although it might sound extreme, I think that the man should talk to a resident assistant about the noisy neighbors. One reason he should do this is that others have already talked to his neighbors about their noisiness, so he has no reason to believe that the neighbors would listen to his requests. Additionally, the man will remain anonymous if he talks to a resident assistant, who has the authority to punish the neighbors for being too loud.

EXERCISE 3

Following the steps below, develop a response to the following prompt.

STEP 1. OUTLINE YOUR RESPONSE

CONVERSATION

FS: *Hey, professor. Can I talk to you for a minute?*

P: *Certainly, Maggie. What can I help you with?*

FS: *I really enjoy your ancient cultures class, and I want to become more involved in archaeology. The problem is that I don't really know how to get involved.*

P: *I'm happy to hear that you'd like to become more involved in archaeology. Well, the best way to become deeply involved in any field is to apply for some internships. In fact, there are several opportunities for internships this summer. Unfortunately, they're unpaid, but they'll provide invaluable experience.*

FS: *Thanks for the recommendation; I'll definitely look into those. But I usually work during the summer to save up money so I can pay for books and tuition. Are there any alternatives?*

P: *Certainly. You could apply to become a teaching assistant for the archaeology department. It won't look as impressive on a resume, but you'll still get to work with some archaeology professors on campus.*

FS: *That sounds like a good idea, too. I'll have to weigh my options carefully. Thanks for your help, professor!*

FS: *Female Student* / **P:** *Professor*

CONVERSATION NOTES

Problem: ______________________________

- **Solution 1:** ______________________________
- **Solution 2:** ______________________________

Prompt

The two students talk about two solutions to the male student's problem. Explain what the male student's problem is. Then state which possible solution you prefer and explain your preference.

STEP 2. PREPARE YOUR RESPONSE

00:00:20

1) Summarize the student's problem.

   From Notes → Problem: ______________________________

2) Identify which of the two proposed solutions your prefer.

   Preferred solution: ______________________________

3) Give two reasons explaining why you prefer this solution.

   Reason 1: ______________________________

   Reason 2: ______________________________

STEP 3. DELIVER YOUR RESPONSE

00:01:00

Response

____

____

____

____

____

____

____

____

____

____

____

Now practice saying your response aloud. If possible, have a friend/classmate fill out this checklist as you say your response to him or her. If you are by yourself, record and listen to your response, and then fill out the checklist below on your own.

Deliver your response within 60 seconds.

Task 5 Response Checklist

	Yes	Somewhat	No
• Does the speaker explain the problem discussed in the conversation?			
• Does the speaker state which of the two proposed solutions he or she prefers?			
• Does the speaker explain why he or she selected this preferred solution?			
• Does the speaker deliver an organized response by using transition words and proper sentence structures?			
• Does the speaker deliver a coherent response by using appropriate tone and pronunciation?			
• Does the speaker finish within the time limit?		X	

CONVERSATION NOTES

Problem: *student wants to be ↑ involved in archae.*

- **Solution 1:** *apply for unpaid summer interns*
- **Solution 2:** *become archae. TA*

1) Summarize the student's problem.

From Notes → Problem: *student wants to be more involved in archaeology*

2) Identify which of the two proposed solutions your prefer.

Preferred solution: *sol. 2*

3) Give two reasons explaining why you prefer this solution.

Reason 1: *she needs summer to save money*

Reason 2: *TA less commitment (good start)*

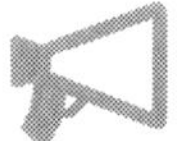

Response

According to the conversation between the professor and the student, the student wants to become more involved in archaeology, but she's not sure how to. The professor recommends that she either apply for some summer internships or try to become an archaeology teaching assistant. I think she should go for the teaching assistant position for a couple of reasons. First, she says that the unpaid summer internships would prevent her from saving money over the summer, which she needs to help pay for school. Thus, pursuing the summer internship seems impractical. Moreover, it sounds like the student is just getting interested in archaeology. If this is true, she should choose the teaching assistant position because it seems like it requires less time and commitment than the internship. Then, if she enjoys being a teaching assistant, she can apply to be an intern next summer instead.

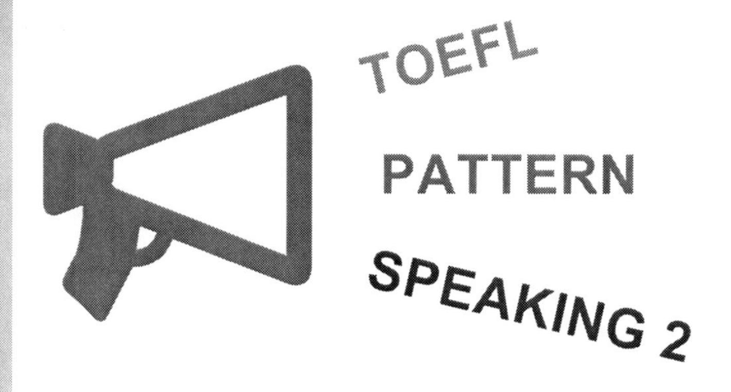

CHAPTER 6

Academic Course
(Listening)

Academic Course: Summarizing

GENERAL BACKGROUND INFORMATION

1. EXPLANATION OF TASK 6

Speaking Task 6 will require you to listen to a brief lecture on an academic subject. The lecture lasts about 90 to 120 seconds and is about 230 to 280 words. The lecture describes a term or concept using academic details or examples. Topics are taken from a range of fields in the life sciences, humanities, social sciences, and physical sciences.

After you listen to the lecture, instructions will inform you to get ready to respond to the question. The prompt will then appear on screen and be read aloud by a narrator.

The task 6 prompt will ask you to describe the main concept or issue of the lecture and use points or examples from the lecture to support the main idea.

Prompt

Using points and examples from the lecture, explain the topic discussed in the lecture.

After listening to the prompt, begin preparing your response. A clock below the prompt will count down. You will have 20 seconds to prepare. At the end, you will hear a short beep.

The clock then changes to "Response Time" and begins to count down. You have 60 seconds to respond. At the end of the 60 seconds, the recording ends and a new message alerts you that the response time is over.

You will need to use citation language, summarizing, paraphrasing, and transitions for this task.

2. NECESSARY SKILLS FOR TASK 6

You must be able to:

- identify and summarize major points from a spoken source of information
- paraphrase information from spoken sources of information
- relate specific examples to a general topic generated from spoken sources of information

HACKING STRATEGY

STEP 1. Outline Your Response

- Take notes as you listen to the lecture
- Read the prompt carefully

STEP 2. Prepare Your Response

- Summarize the lecture's main idea
- State how the examples in the lecture relate to the main idea or to each other

STEP 3. Deliver Your Response

- Respond with coherent sentences
- Add transition words between ideas

STEP 1. OUTLINE YOUR RESPONSE

Take notes on important information as you listen to the lecture. Do not take notes using full sentences, as you will not have time to do so.

LECTURE

Lipoproteins

Cholesterol is a fat-like substance that travels in the bloodstream. It's carried along in the blood inside of protein "packages" called lipoproteins. These lipoproteins have different effects on the body depending on how they're "packed," so to speak.

If they are low-density lipoproteins, or LDLs, the particles may be harmful. Some smaller LDLs can attach to the walls of the arteries, building up a hard crust. Doctors call the hard crust "plaque." A build-up of plaque is dangerous because it may cause heart attack or stroke if it affects blood's ability to flow by blocking the arteries.

If the lipoprotein particle is very dense – a high-density lipoprotein (HDL) – it may help prevent plaque from forming. Some HDL particles carry away extra LDL particles, transporting them to the liver, where the cholesterol can begin to be processed out of the body.

LECTURE NOTES

Main Idea: *lipoproteins = packages carrying cholest.*

- **Subtopic 1:** *LDL = harmful*

  Details: *plaque/arteries, build-up → heart attack, stroke*

- **Subtopic 2:** *HDL = helpful*

  Details: *carries cholest. from heart → liver → out of body*

After taking notes, carefully read the prompt, making sure that you know exactly what it asks you to do.

Prompt

Using points and details from the lecture, describe two types of lipoproteins.

STEP 2. PREPARE YOUR RESPONSE

During the 20-second preparation time, make sure that your notes address all the points in the prompt, and use the information in your notes to organize your response. Because you have so little time to prepare your response, do not write complete sentences.

1) Make sure that you can summarize the main idea of the lecture.
 From Notes → Main Idea: *lipoproteins = packages carrying cholesterol*

2) Make sure that you can explain the first subtopic presented in the lecture.
 From Notes → Subtopic 1: *LDL = harmful*
 causes plaque in arteries, build-up → heart attack, stroke

3) Make sure that you can explain the second subtopic presented in the lecture.
 From Notes → Subtopic 2: *HDL = helpful*
 carries cholesterol from heart → liver → out of body

STEP 3. DELIVER YOUR RESPONSE

Use the outline that you created in STEP 2 to guide you as you deliver your response. Respond using complete sentences, and add transition words to show how ideas relate to one another.

Lipoproteins carry cholesterol in the blood. The professor describes two types of lipoproteins: low-density, called "LDLs," some of which are harmful, and high-density, called "HDLs." The smaller types of LDLs are especially bad because they can form plaque along the walls of a person's arteries. When the plaque builds up, people run a high risk of heart attack and stroke. However, the other kind of lipoprotein, HDL, helps prevent the build-up of plaque. HDL particles do this by carrying LDL particles from the heart to the liver, where they can be broken down and ejected from the body.

STEP 1. OUTLINE YOUR RESPONSE

NOTE-TAKING STRATEGIES

Taking notes quickly during the listening portion of this task is crucial, as you can use your notes to help outline your speaking response. When taking notes, you should be able to **abbreviate**, or shorten, common words or phrases and **condense information** in order to save time.

Tips for taking notes:

- Only write down key points/information that you will use in your response.
- Because of time constraints, do not write using full sentences.
- Make sure that you can understand your own abbreviations.

TAKING NOTES ON THE LECTURE

When taking notes on the lecture, be sure to identify the **main idea** of the lecture. Then take notes on the **two subtopics** that relate to or elaborate on the main idea.

LECTURE

Reptiles and Amphibians

Reptiles, such as lizards, and amphibians, such as frogs, are distantly related. However, one major difference is that amphibians are more adapted to an aquatic environment.

Reptiles hatch from hard-shelled eggs on dry land; they breathe through their lungs right away. In contrast, amphibians hatch underwater, where they begin their lives as fish-like creatures, breathing through gills. Later, amphibians change form and develop lungs, allowing them to walk on land.

Another major difference between reptiles and amphibians is their skins. Even though most amphibians can live out of the water, they still have soft, thin skin that must be kept moist. Their thin skin is able to absorb oxygen when they're underwater, so they can stay submerged. Reptiles have a thicker skin; they can't breathe through it underwater, but it protects them on dry land.

LECTURE NOTES

Main Idea: *diff. b/w reptiles & amphibians*

- **Subtopic 1:** *reptile characteristics*

  Details: *hatch on land, breathe w/ lungs, thick, protective skin*

- **Subtopic 2:** *amphibian characteristics*

  Details: *hatch in H_2O, breathe w/ gills/lungs, soft skin for ox. absorption*

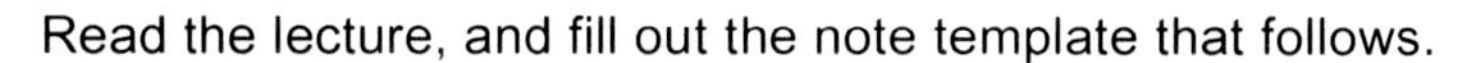

Read the lecture, and fill out the note template that follows.

LECTURE

Bird Nests

When most of us think of a bird's nest, we probably picture a round basket-like structure found in a tree. However, many bird species have developed incredibly diverse nesting strategies for keeping their eggs warm and safe.

At one extreme is the Emperor Penguin, which doesn't build a nest at all. The female lays one egg and then leaves for two months to find food. The male penguin keeps the egg balanced on his feet and covered under a warm layer of his skin until the egg hatches.

At the other extreme is the Australian malleefowl. The male digs a wide, deep hole and fills it with organic material and sand. Gradually the materials form a mound and generate heat as they break down. When the mound is warm enough inside, the female digs into it, lays her eggs, and covers them. The male and female monitor the mound. They add or remove material to keep the mound at just the right temperature until the eggs hatch. The process may take up most of a year.

LECTURE NOTES

Main Idea: ______________________________

- Subtopic 1: ______________________________

  ____

- Subtopic 2: ______________________________

  ____

STEP 2. PREPARE YOUR RESPONSE

LECTURE

Reptiles and Amphibians

Reptiles, such as lizards, and amphibians, such as frogs, are distantly related. However, one major difference is that amphibians are more adapted to an aquatic environment.

Reptiles hatch from hard-shelled eggs on dry land; they breathe through their lungs right away. In contrast, amphibians hatch underwater, where they begin their lives as fish-like creatures, breathing through gills. Later, amphibians change form and develop lungs, allowing them to walk on land.

Another major difference between reptiles and amphibians is their skins. Even though most amphibians can live out of the water, they still have soft, thin skin that must be kept moist. Their thin skin is able to absorb oxygen when they're underwater, so they can stay submerged. Reptiles have a thicker skin; they can't breathe through it underwater, but it protects them on dry land.

LECTURE NOTES

Main Idea: *diff. b/w reptiles & amphibians*

- **Subtopic 1:** *reptile characteristics*
  Details: *hatch on land, breathe w/ lungs, thick, protective skin*
- **Subtopic 2:** *amphibian characteristics*
  Details: *hatch in H_2O, breathe w/ gills/lungs, soft skin for ox. absorption*

After taking notes on the lecture, carefully read the prompt that appears on the screen. Make sure that you understand exactly what the prompt is asking you to do.

Prompt

Using points and examples from the talk, describe some differences between reptiles and amphibians.

After reading the prompt, you have 20 seconds to prepare your response. During your preparation time, organize your notes so you can address the following pieces of information in your response.

1) Make sure that you can summarize the main idea of the lecture.

   From Notes → Main Idea: *difference between reptiles and amphibians*

2) Make sure that you can explain the first subtopic presented in the lecture.

   From Notes → Subtopic 1: *reptile characteristics*
   hatch on land, breath with lungs, protected with thick skin

3) Make sure that you can explain the second subtopic presented in the lecture.

   From Notes → Subtopic 2: *amphibian characteristics*
   hatch in water, breathe using gills (young)/lungs (grown),
   absorb oxygen through soft skin

Review the following lecture. Then prepare a Task 6 response, using the template below. Review your notes from the previous page if necessary.

LECTURE

Bird Nests

When most of us think of a bird's nest, we probably picture a round basket-like structure found in a tree. However, many bird species have developed incredibly diverse nesting strategies for keeping their eggs warm and safe.

At one extreme is the Emperor Penguin, which doesn't build a nest at all. The female lays one egg and then leaves for two months to find food. The male penguin keeps the egg balanced on his feet and covered under a warm layer of his skin until the egg hatches.

At the other extreme is the Australian malleefowl. The male digs a wide, deep hole and fills it with organic material and sand. Gradually the materials form a mound and generate heat as they break down. When the mound is warm enough inside, the female digs into it, lays her eggs, and covers them. The male and female monitor the mound. They add or remove material to keep the mound at just the right temperature until the eggs hatch. The process may take up most of a year.

Prompt

Using the examples mentioned by the professor, describe two unusual bird-nesting strategies.

1) Summarize the main idea of the lecture.

From Notes → Main Idea: ____________________

2) Explain the first subtopic presented in the lecture.

From Notes → Subtopic 1: ____________________

Details: ____________________

____

3) Explain the second subtopic presented in the lecture.

From Notes → Subtopic 2: ____________________

Details: ____________________

____

STEP 3. DELIVER YOUR RESPONSE

Use the outline that you created in STEP 2 to guide you as you respond to the prompt.

Prompt

Using points and examples from the talk, describe some differences between reptiles and amphibians.

- **Lecture Main Idea:** The first sentence of your response should be a summary of the main idea from the lecture.
- **Summary of Subtopic 1:** Then describe the first subtopic of the lecture, being sure to relate it to the main idea.
- **Summary of Subtopic 2:** Lastly, describe the second subtopic, being sure to relate it to the rest of the lecture information.
- Include **transition words** in your response to clarify the relationships between related ideas.

Example Response

	Notes		Response
Lecture Main Idea	*diff. b/w reptiles & amphibians*	→	*The lecture describes several differences between reptiles and amphibians, which are distantly related to one another.*
Summary of Subtopic 1	*reptiles → hatch on land, breath w/ lungs, protected w/ thick skin*	→	*Several qualities are unique to reptiles.* ***First****, reptiles hatch on land, which means they breathe using lungs from birth.* ***Moreover****, they're protected by thick skin.*
Summary of Subtopic 2	*amphibians→ hatch in H_2O, breathe using gills (young)/ lungs (grown), absorb ox. through soft skin*	→	***But*** *amphibians hatch in water, so they're born with gills. They develop lungs later in life, so they can live on land, too.* ***Furthermore****, amphibians have soft skin that allows them to absorb oxygen through their skin when they're underwater.*

Review the following lecture and prompt. Then write a Task 6 response. Review your notes from the previous practices if necessary. Once you have written down your response, **say it aloud to yourself, a friend, a classmate, or a family member**.

LECTURE

Bird Nests

When most of us think of a bird's nest, we probably picture a round basket-like structure found in a tree. However, many bird species have developed incredibly diverse nesting strategies for keeping their eggs warm and safe.

At one extreme is the Emperor Penguin, which doesn't build a nest at all. The female lays one egg and then leaves for two months to find food. The male penguin keeps the egg balanced on his feet and covered under a warm layer of his skin until the egg hatches.

At the other extreme is the Australian malleefowl. The male digs a wide, deep hole and fills it with organic material and sand. Gradually the materials form a mound and generate heat as they break down. When the mound is warm enough inside, the female digs into it, lays her eggs, and covers them. The male and female monitor the mound. They add or remove material to keep the mound at just the right temperature until the eggs hatch. The process may take up most of a year.

Prompt

Using the examples mentioned by the professor, describe two unusual bird-nesting strategies.

Response

EXERCISE 1

Following the steps below, develop a response to the following prompt.

STEP 1. OUTLINE YOUR RESPONSE

LECTURE

Stocks

Today I'll talk about stocks – one of the primary ways of making money in the corporate world. In effect, stocks allow people to own a part of a corporation. Let's learn about the distinctions between two types of stock – common stock and preferred stock. Each of these types of stocks has its own advantages and disadvantages.

People who buy common stock in a company have the chance of earning more money. If the company makes a profit and grows, common stockholders will earn higher "dividends," which are cash payments that are distributed every few months. Common stockholders also get to have some say in how the company is run by voting to elect company directors. A disadvantage is that if the company doesn't succeed, common stockholders stand to lose everything they invested.

Preferred stockholders have the advantage of a more stable investment. They get paid dividends at a fixed rate, assuming the company does not go bankrupt. Even if the company does go out of business, preferred stockholders will get any remaining dividends before common stockholders do, because they're "preferred." However, disadvantages include not having any say in company elections, and not getting any increased payments or value if the company grows and profits increase.

LECTURE NOTES

Main Idea: ______________________________

- Subtopic 1: ______________________________

  Details: ______________________________

  ____

- Subtopic 2: ______________________________

  Details: ______________________________

  ____

Prompt

Using points and details from the lecture, explain some similarities and differences between common and preferred stocks.

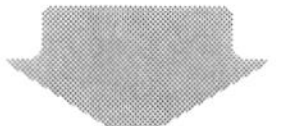

STEP 2. Prepare Your Response

00:00:20

1) Summarize the main idea of the lecture.

   From Notes → Main Idea: ______________________________

2) Explain the first subtopic presented in the lecture.

   From Notes → Subtopic 1: ______________________________

   ____

3) Explain the second subtopic presented in the lecture.

   From Notes → Subtopic 2: ______________________________

   ____

STEP 3. Deliver Your Response

00:01:00

Response

____

____

____

____

____

____

____

____

Now practice saying your response aloud. If possible, have a friend/classmate fill out this checklist as you say your response to him or her. If you are by yourself, record and listen to your response, and then fill out the checklist below on your own.

Deliver your response within 60 seconds.

Task 6 Response Checklist

	Yes	Somewhat	No
• Does the speaker briefly describe the main concept of the lecture?			
• Does the speaker summarize the two examples/topics that elaborate on the lecture's main concepts?			
• Does the speaker explain how these two examples/ topics relate to one another?			
• Does the speaker deliver an organized response by using transition words and proper sentence structures?			
• Does the speaker deliver a coherent response by using appropriate tone and pronunciation?			
• Does the speaker finish within the time limit?		X	

LECTURE NOTES

Main Idea: *stocks (owning pt. of a corp.)*

- Subtopic 1: *common stock*

  Details: *(+) vote on company's decisions, get earnings reports*

  (-) last to get profits on company's earnings

- Subtopic 2: *preferred stock*

  Details: *(+) get profits 1st, get + dividends*

  (-) no say in company's decisions

1) Summarize the main idea of the lecture.

   From Notes → Main Idea: *stocks (owning part of a corporation)*

2) Explain the first subtopic presented in the lecture.

   From Notes → Subtopic 1: *common stock*

   (+) potential to earn more money, vote; (-) might lose money if company does

3) Explain the second subtopic presented in the lecture.

   From Notes → Subtopic 2: *preferred stock*

   (+) stable, fixed payments, first to get paid; (-) less chance to make money

Response

The lecture discusses different types of investment in companies. Both common stock and preferred stock allow buyers to own a small part of a company. The difference is that common stock allows buyers to take more of a risk. The company may pay them higher or lower dividends as its profits go up and down. If the company fails, common stockholders may get nothing. Perhaps because of the greater risk, common stock holders get to vote on who leads the company. Preferred stocks offer a safer investment. Preferred stockholders get exactly the same dividends each time they're given out. If the company fails, they're "preferred" to get any money that's left. But the disadvantage is that if the company's profits grow, preferred stockholders don't see an increase in payments.

EXERCISE 2

Following the steps below, develop a response to the following prompt.

STEP 1. Outline Your Response

LECTURE

Eyes and Sunlight

So as you have probably heard before, medical researchers have found that exposure to sunshine is important for health in several ways. But overexposure to the sun can be harmful, too. Human skin and eyes need to absorb some sunlight, but how much? This is an enormous topic, so today I'd like to focus on just the good and bad long-term effects of sunlight on children's eyes.

First, the good: it turns out that outdoor light helps vision develop properly. Studies from many countries indicate that children who spend about two hours a day outdoors have a dramatically improved chance of maintaining good eyesight. The explanation may be that bright outdoor light stimulates the creation of dopamine, a hormone that regulates the growth of the eye's retina, its innermost layer. When deprived of dopamine, the retina grows too long and can't transmit clear images without glasses.

On the other hand, children's eyes can suffer harm later in life from exposure to the ultraviolet rays in sunshine. These UV rays are the same rays that cause sunburn on the skin. Eyes can be doubly affected by UV rays if the rays reflect off of water, sand, or snow. UV rays are thought to cause cataracts, cancers, and pterygium (tur-RIDGE-ium) – often called "surfer's eye" – a non-cancerous pink growth on the white part of the eye.

LECTURE NOTES

Main Idea: ______________________________

- Subtopic 1: ______________________________

  Details: ______________________________

  ____

- Subtopic 2: ______________________________

  Details: ______________________________

  ____

Prompt

Using points and details from the lecture, summarize the effects of sunlight on the human eye.

STEP 2. PREPARE YOUR RESPONSE

00:00:20

1) Summarize the main idea of the lecture.

From Notes → Main Idea: ______________________________

2) Explain the first subtopic presented in the lecture.

From Notes → Subtopic 1: ______________________________

____

3) Explain the second subtopic presented in the lecture.

From Notes → Subtopic 2: ______________________________

____

STEP 3. DELIVER YOUR RESPONSE

00:01:00

Response

____

____

____

____

____

____

____

____

Now practice saying your response aloud. If possible, have a friend/classmate fill out this checklist as you say your response to him or her. If you are by yourself, record and listen to your response, and then fill out the checklist below on your own.

Deliver your response within 60 seconds.

Task 6 Response Checklist

	Yes	Somewhat	No
• Does the speaker briefly describe the main concept of the lecture?			
• Does the speaker summarize the two examples/topics that elaborate on the lecture's main concepts?			
• Does the speaker explain how these two examples/ topics relate to one another?			
• Does the speaker deliver an organized response by using transition words and proper sentence structures?			
• Does the speaker deliver a coherent response by using appropriate tone and pronunciation?			
• Does the speaker finish within the time limit?		X	

LECTURE NOTES

Main Idea: *sunshine helps/harms children's eyes*

- Subtopic 1: *outdoor light for 2+ hr./day → good vision*

  Details: *bright light ↑ dopamine (controls retina growth)*

- Subtopic 2: *UV rays → harm later, esp. if reflected*

  Details: *cataracts, cancers, surfer's eye*

1) Summarize the main idea of the lecture.

From Notes → Main Idea: *sunshine helps/harms humans, including eye development*

2) Explain the first subtopic presented in the lecture.

From Notes → Subtopic 1: *outdoor light for 2 or more hours per day develops good vision*

bright light increases dopamine (controls retina growth)

3) Explain the second subtopic presented in the lecture.

From Notes → Subtopic 2: *UV rays cause harm later in life, especially if reflected*

examples include cataracts, cancers, surfer's eye

Response

The professor talks about the positive and negative effects that sunlight has on people's health. He focuses on sunlight's effects on children's eyes. First, he describes how researchers from around the world are finding that it's important for children to be outdoors in the light, even just for two hours a day, in order to have the best chance for good eyesight into adulthood. One reason may be that outdoor light causes the body to release dopamine, a chemical that helps shape the inner part of the eye. Secondly, the professor talks about the danger of the UV rays in sunshine. They can cause damage that shows up later, especially if they're also reflected back up by water, sand, or snow. UV rays may be the cause of cataracts, cancers, and "surfer's eye," so they're very dangerous.

EXERCISE 3

Following the steps below, develop a response to the following prompt.

STEP 1. OUTLINE YOUR RESPONSE

LECTURE

Fear and Censorship

From 1917 to 1921, United States politics revolved around fear. The U.S. public had a lot to be afraid of; this time period included major global conflicts, a worldwide influenza outbreak, letter-bombs sent by terrorists in the U.S., a new ban on alcohol, the rise of violent racist groups, and an economic recession. And on top of all these political and social issues, all branches of government repressed free speech in America at this time. Post offices refused to deliver certain publications, and political protesters were imprisoned. Let's look at two main reasons for America's period of intense censorship.

First, Americans had to be persuaded to get involved in the brutal World War I in Europe. When the U.S. finally entered the war in 1917, not enough American men volunteered, so President Woodrow Wilson started a military draft. It was the first time the U.S. had tried to force millions of men to serve in the military, so Wilson combined it with a propaganda campaign. During this time of hyper-patriotic campaigning, Congress passed a law that made "disloyal" speech a federal crime.

The second reason was that Americans feared that communists were secretly entering the U.S. with the intent of overthrowing democracy. Russia was experiencing a socialist revolution. Mexico's civil war also seemed to have socialist factions. In 1920, the U.S. attorney general put the U.S. on alert for a rumored socialist uprising on May 1. When nothing happened on that day, many Americans relaxed. By the end of the year, censorship finally ended.

LECTURE NOTES

Main Idea: ______________________________

- Subtopic 1: ______________________________

  Details: ______________________________

  ____

- Subtopic 2: ______________________________

  Details: ______________________________

  ____

Prompt

The professor discusses censorship in early 20th-century America. Summarize the two main causes of censorship discussed in the lecture.

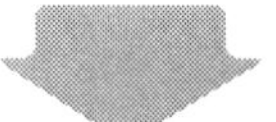

STEP 2. PREPARE YOUR RESPONSE

00:00:20

1) Summarize the main idea of the lecture.

From Notes → Main Idea: ______________________________

2) Explain the first subtopic presented in the lecture.

From Notes → Subtopic 1: ______________________________

____

3) Explain the second subtopic presented in the lecture.

From Notes → Subtopic 2: ______________________________

____

STEP 3. DELIVER YOUR RESPONSE

00:01:00

Response

____

____

____

____

____

____

____

____

Now practice saying your response aloud. If possible, have a friend/classmate fill out this checklist as you say your response to him or her. If you are by yourself, record and listen to your response, and then fill out the checklist below on your own.

Deliver your response within 60 seconds.

Task 6 Response Checklist

	Yes	Somewhat	No
• Does the speaker briefly describe the main concept of the lecture?			
• Does the speaker summarize the two examples/topics that elaborate on the lecture's main concepts?			
• Does the speaker explain how these two examples/topics relate to one another?			
• Does the speaker deliver an organized response by using transition words and proper sentence structures?			
• Does the speaker deliver a coherent response by using appropriate tone and pronunciation?			
• Does the speaker finish within the time limit?		X	

LECTURE NOTES

Main Idea: *U.S. fear (1917-1921) → censorship*

- Subtopic 1: *WWI unpopular → military draft*

  Details: *draft → propaganda, disloyal speech = crime*

- Subtopic 2: *U.S. feared Russian/Mexican socialism*

  Details: *Amer. feared revolution in U.S.; no revolution → U.S. relaxed*

1) Summarize the main idea of the lecture.

   From Notes → Main Idea: *U.S. fear from 1917 to 1921 → censorship*

2) Explain the first subtopic presented in the lecture.

   From Notes → Subtopic 1: *World War I unpopular → military draft*

   draft led to propaganda, disloyal speech became a crime

3) Explain the second subtopic presented in the lecture.

   From Notes → Subtopic 2: *U.S. feared Russian/Mexican socialism would overthrow government*

   Americans feared revolution in U.S.; no revolution → U.S. relaxed

Response

The lecture talks about American history from 1917 to 1921. At this time, Americans feared things such as political change and disease. On top of all this, the U.S. government actually put people in prison for speaking out and stopped some publications at post offices. According to the lecture, one main reason is that the government was having a hard time getting public support for drafting soldiers to fight in World War I. The censorship was the other side of the government's public relations effort. Another reason was that, with revolutions going on in Russia and Mexico, Americans feared a socialist takeover in the U.S. When it didn't happen, the tension eased, and the government ended censorship.

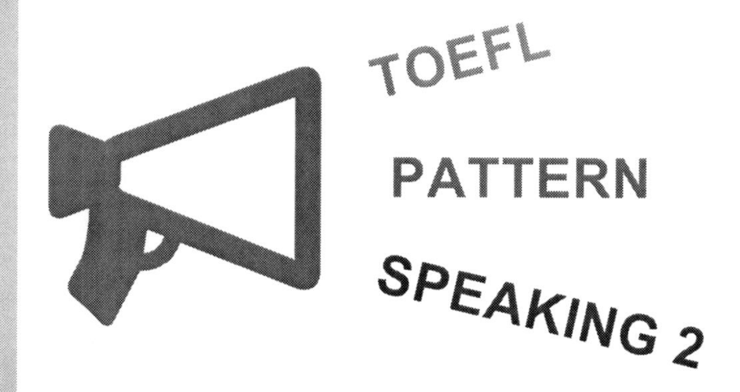

CHAPTER 7

Actual Practice

TOEFL iBT Independent Speaking Task Rubric (Tasks 1-2)

4	**OVERVIEW** • ***Although the response may include brief lapses* in clarity, the vast majority of the response is intelligible and comprehensive. For a response to receive a score of 4, it must accomplish all of the following:*** **SPEECH** • The speaker delivers an articulate response that requires little to no interpretation on the part of the listener. Any mistakes or omissions do not affect the listener's ability to comprehend the speaker's response. **VOCABULARY AND GRAMMAR** • The speaker demonstrates his or her command of a sophisticated vocabulary and an understanding of various sentence structures. Minimal pauses indicate a strong familiarity with the English language. Any vocabulary or grammar mistakes do not affect the listener's ability to understand the response. **CONTENT** • The speaker completely addresses all aspects of the prompt by presenting ideas in a logical and organized manner.
3	**OVERVIEW** • ***The response may contain noticeable lapses in clarity and organization, but it is still consistently intelligible and exhibits a clear understanding of the prompt. for a response to receive a score of 3, it must accomplish at least two of the following:*** **SPEECH** • The speaker delivers a response that is generally comprehensible, but noticeable pronunciation or inflection issues may occasionally obscure the speaker's meaning. **VOCABULARY AND GRAMMAR** • Although the speaker's grasp of vocabulary and grammar structures may be somewhat limited and occasionally inaccurate, any errors or mistakes do not greatly interfere with the speaker's overall ability to respond to the prompt. **CONTENT** • The speaker addresses all aspects of the prompt, even though the response may lack detailed explanations and may contain lapses in organization.

***Lapse**: a temporary decline in quality of something

<table>
<tr><td>2</td><td>

OVERVIEW

- ***The response includes information relevant to the prompt, but the listener's comprehension is hindered by frequent lapses in the speaker's fluency. For a response to receive a score of 2, it must accomplish at least two of the following:***

SPEECH

- The speaker delivers a response that requires active interpretation on the part of the listener. Although most of the response is intelligible, frequent pronunciation and inflection issues obscure the speaker's meaning.

VOCABULARY AND GRAMMAR

- A limited grasp of vocabulary and grammar structures often prevents the speaker from fully articulating his or her thoughts. The response is dominated by short, simple sentences and is characterized by a limited vocabulary.

CONTENT

- The response generally connects to the prompt, but it lacks details and examples. The few details and examples that are presented may be unclear or redundant.

</td></tr>
<tr><td>1</td><td>

OVERVIEW

- ***The response barely addresses the prompt, and/or the majority of the response is incomprehensible. For a response to receive a score of 1, it must accomplish at least two of the following:***

SPEECH

- Frequent and reoccurring pronunciation and inflection issues make most of the response difficult to understand, if not entirely incomprehensible. Constant interpretation is required on the part of the listener.

VOCABULARY AND GRAMMAR

- A limited grasp of vocabulary and grammar prevents the speaker from articulating his or her thoughts. The speaker may rely heavily on clichés or memorized phrases and expressions.

CONTENT

- The speaker conveys little information that is relevant to the prompt. Only simple ideas are presented, and these ideas may be unclear or redundant.

</td></tr>
<tr><td>0</td><td>

OVERVIEW

- ***The speaker does not respond to the prompt. The speaker may deliver a response that is unrelated to the prompt, or the speaker may deliver a response in a language other than English.***

</td></tr>
</table>

TOEFL iBT Integrated Speaking Task Rubric (Tasks 3-6)

<table>
<tr><td>4</td><td>

OVERVIEW

- ***The speaker addresses all aspects of the prompt. Despite infrequent lapses in clarity, the response is intelligible and comprehensive. For a response to a receive a score of 4, it must address all of the following:***

SPEECH

- The speaker may pause in order to recall or reference information, but these pauses do not affect the listener's comprehension. Similarly, any mistakes or omissions do not affect the listener's ability to comprehend the speaker's response.

VOCABULARY AND GRAMMAR

- The speaker demonstrates his or her command of a sophisticated vocabulary and an understanding of various sentence structures. Minimal pauses indicate a strong familiarity with the English language. Any vocabulary or grammar mistakes do not affect the listener's ability to understand the response. The speaker uses nearly all relevant terms from the listening and/or reading portions of the task.

CONTENT

- The speaker organizes and presents nearly all relevant information presented in the task. The relationships between ideas are consistently clear.

</td></tr>
<tr><td>3</td><td>

OVERVIEW

- ***The response may contain noticeable lapses in clarity and organization, but it is still consistently intelligible and exhibits a clear understanding of the requirements of the task. For a response to receive a score of 3, it must accomplish at least two of the following:***

SPEECH

- The speaker delivers a response that is generally comprehensible, but noticeable pronunciation or inflection issues may occasionally interfere with the speaker's ability to convey information presented in the task.

VOCABULARY AND GRAMMAR

- Although the speaker's grasp of vocabulary and grammar structures may be somewhat limited and occasionally inaccurate, any errors or mistakes do not greatly interfere with the speaker's overall ability to form a response. The speaker uses some relevant terms from the listening and/or reading portions of the task.

CONTENT

- The speaker addresses most of the relevant information presented in the task, but the response may be missing some details, contain some inaccurate information, or include lapses in organization and clarity.

</td></tr>
</table>

Score	Description
2	**OVERVIEW** • ***The response includes information relevant to the task, but some information may be inaccurate or omitted altogether. A lack of clarity or intelligibility may interfere with the listener's comprehension of the response. For a response to receive a score of 2, it must accomplish at least two of the following:*** **SPEECH** • The speaker delivers a response that requires active interpretation on the part of the listener. Although most of the response is intelligible, frequent pronunciation and inflection issues obscure the speaker's meaning. **VOCABULARY AND GRAMMAR** • A limited grasp of vocabulary and grammar structures often prevent the speaker from fully articulating his or her thoughts. The response is dominated by short, simple sentences and is characterized by a limited vocabulary. The speaker uses few relevant terms from the listening and/or reading portions of the task. **CONTENT** • The response relates to the information presented in the task, but it contains many obvious omissions or inaccuracies. Any main ideas are explained vaguely or inaccurately, and main ideas may be confused with minor details or irrelevant information presented in the listening and/or reading portions of the task.
1	**OVERVIEW** • ***The response includes very few pieces of information that are relevant to the task, and/or the majority of the response is incomprehensible. For a response to receive a score of 1, it must accomplish at least two of the following:*** **SPEECH** • Frequent and reoccurring pronunciation and inflection issues make most of the response difficult to understand, if not entirely incomprehensible. Constant interpretation is required on the part of the listener. **VOCABULARY AND GRAMMAR** • A limited grasp of vocabulary and grammar prevents the speaker from articulating his or her thoughts. The speaker may rely heavily on clichés or memorized phrases and expressions. The speaker does not use any relevant terms from the listening and/or reading portions of the task. **CONTENT** • The speaker conveys little information that is relevant to the information presented in the task. Only simple ideas are presented, and these ideas may be unclear or redundant.
0	**OVERVIEW** • ***The speaker does not respond to the prompt. The speaker may deliver a response that is unrelated to the prompt, or the speaker may deliver a response in a language other than English.***

TASK 1

ACTUAL PRACTICE 1

Prompt

Name a country that you would like to visit. Explain why you would like to travel to this place and include details and examples to support your response.

Preparation Time 00:00:15
Response Time 00:00:45

Notes

Opinion: ____________________

- ____________________
- ____________________

Response

____

Prompt

Some people believe that success is achieved through hard work and dedication, while other people believe that success is mostly decided through luck and good fortune. Which opinion do you believe and why? Use specific reasons in your answer.

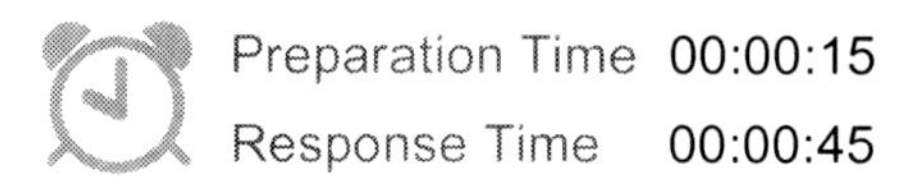

Notes

Preference: ______________________________

- ______________________________
- ______________________________

Response

____

____

____

____

____

____

____

____

____

____

TASK 1

Model Answer

Prompt

Name a country that you would like to visit. Explain why you would like to travel to this place and include details and examples to support you explanation.

Notes

Opinion: *visit Italy*

- *many historical sites*
- *beautiful scenery*

Response

If I had the opportunity to visit any country, I'd choose to visit Italy for a number of reasons. For one, I'd love to visit some of the many historical sites in Italy. Because I've studied Greek and Roman history for many years, seeing Roman monuments such as the Pantheon and the Coliseum has been a lifelong dream of mine. Moreover, Italy has diverse geography, so visiting the sunny beaches in the southern part of Italy or journeying to the Alps in the north would be interesting and enjoyable.

Model Answer

Prompt

Some people believe that success is achieved through hard work and dedication, while other people believe that success is mostly decided through luck and good fortune. Which opinion do you believe and why? Use specific reasons in your answer.

Notes

Preference: *hard work/dedication = success*

- *puts me in control of my fate*
- *optimistic → anything becomes possible*

Response

Although some people believe that success comes from luck, I believe that usually, success comes from hard work and dedication. For one, this belief puts me in control of my own fate. When I want something, I feel that the best way to get it is to make a plan and work hard to accomplish that plan. Moreover, believing that success comes from hard work makes me optimistic; anything is achievable if I work hard enough to attain it. For example, when I first tried to join the basketball team, I didn't make the team because I was too short. So I practiced for a whole year, and when I tried out a second time, my skills had improved so much that I made the team despite my height; luck had little to do with my success.

UNIVERSITY ANNOUNCEMENT

Physical Education Requirements

Starting next academic year, State University will require all students to take one year of physical education classes. These classes will be graded using the pass/no pass system. The physical education department will offer a wide variety of classes, including dance, yoga, martial arts, and various team sports. The university hopes that this new requirement will inspire more socializing, provide an opportunity for students to relieve stress from academic courses, and encourage interest in the school's comprehensive recreational facilities.

Announcement Notes

Proposal: ______________________________

- ______________________________
- ______________________________

CONVERSATION

M: *I'm really excited about the new physical education requirement.*

F: *Really? I'm not so sure about it myself. Why are you so excited?*

M: *Well, like the announcement says, I think it'll get students to be more social. These athletic classes will have students from a bunch of different majors, and it'll be nice to meet people who study different subjects.*

F: *That's true. Most of my friends are in the same major as me. It'll be exciting to meet people with different academic interests.*

M: *Exactly! And this new requirement will force me to get some more exercise. I'd really like to slim down because I've gained a lot of weight since the beginning of the year.*

F: *I'm with you there. Must be all that dining hall food (laughs).*

M: *Male Student* / **F:** *Female Student*

Conversation Notes

Speaker's opinion: ______________________________

- ______________________________
- ______________________________

Prompt

The man expresses his opinion about the plan described in the announcement. Briefly summarize the plan. Then state his opinion about the plan and explain the reasons he gives for holding that opinion.

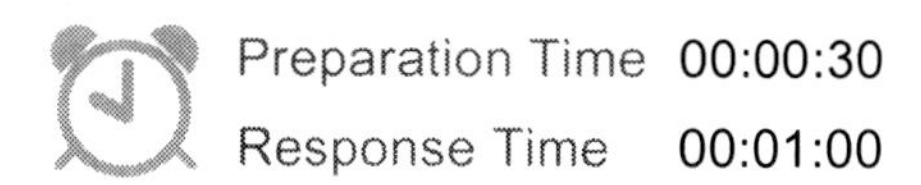

Use your 30 seconds of "Preparation Time" to organize your notes and prepare for your response.

Write your response on the lines below. Then **say your response aloud**, making sure that you can deliver your response within 1 minute.

Response

Model Answer

UNIVERSITY ANNOUNCEMENT

Physical Education Requirements

Starting next academic year, State University will require all students to take one year of physical education classes. These classes will be graded using the pass/no pass system. The physical education department will offer a wide variety of classes, including dance, yoga, martial arts, and various team sports. The university hopes that this new requirement will inspire more socializing, provide an opportunity for students to relieve stress from academic courses, and encourage interest in the school's comprehensive recreational facilities.

Announcement Notes

Proposal: *require 1 yr. of PE classes*

- *encourage socializing*
- *relieve academic stress*

CONVERSATION

M: *I'm really excited about the new physical education requirement.*

F: *Really? I'm not so sure about it myself. Why are you so excited?*

M: *Well, like the announcement says, I think it'll get students to be more social. These athletic classes will have students from a bunch of different majors, and it'll be nice to meet people who study different subjects.*

F: *That's true. Most of my friends are in the same major as me. It'll be exciting to meet people with different academic interests.*

M: *Exactly! And this new requirement will force me to get some more exercise. I'd really like to slim down because I've gained a lot of weight since the beginning of the year.*

F: *I'm with you there. Must be all that dining hall food* (laughs).

M: *Male Student* / **F:** *Female Student*

Conversation Notes

Speaker's opinion: *man supports*

- *meet diff. ppl. (socialize)*
- *more exercise (stop weight gain)*

Prompt

The man expresses his opinion about the plan described in the announcement. Briefly summarize the plan. Then state his opinion about the plan and explain the reasons he gives for holding that opinion.

Response

The university announcement states that, starting next year, students will have to take a year of physical education classes in order to graduate. The man supports this proposal for a couple of reasons. First, he agrees with the announcement's claim that the physical education classes will bring students from many different majors together. Thus, he thinks that he'll be able to meet people in the physical education classes that he wouldn't meet otherwise. Additionally, the male student believes that this new requirement will force him to start exercising more. He wants to lose some weight because he says that he's gained weight recently.

PASSAGE

Melodrama

A *melodrama* is a narrative that depicts characters and events that are exaggerated to appeal to audiences' emotions. Generally, characters in melodramas are extremely moral or immoral, and the plot is fast paced. Melodramas usually place these unrealistic characters and events in realistic settings, making the stories more relatable to audiences. Melodramas have existed since the 18th century, and the style has remained popular because melodramas allow audiences to escape from reality by engaging themselves in larger-than-life characters, emotions, and events.

Passage Notes

Main Idea: ______________________________

- ______________________________
- ______________________________

LECTURE

Popular culture often blends elements of melodrama with different genres. Now let's look at two examples of this blending: the 1939 American film Gone with the Wind *and the 2013 South Korean television show* My Love from the Star.

Adapted from the 1936 novel of the same name, Gone with the Wind *takes place in the southern United States during and after the American Civil War. The story follows Scarlett O'Hara, the daughter of a wealthy plantation owner, as she struggles to survive the destructive wake of the Civil War. The film uses melodramatic elements such as exaggerated characters, obsession, and a war-zone setting. Audiences and critics loved the mixture of melodrama and history, and the film was a huge box-office success.*

For a more recent example of melodrama, let's discuss the Korean show My Love from the Star. *The show follows a handsome alien who becomes stranded on Earth for centuries before falling in love with a beautiful actress. This show takes a science fiction plot — an alien being stranded on Earth — and adds many elements of melodrama: the plot centers on romance, and there are clear divisions between the good and evil characters. Mixing science fiction and melodrama has proven successful, as the show has become popular both in South Korea and abroad.*

Lecture Notes

Topic: ______________________________

Example 1: ______________________________

- Details: ______________________________

Example 2: ______________________________

- Details: ______________________________

Prompt

Using details and examples from both the passage and the lecture, describe some qualities of melodramas and explain how they are used in film and television

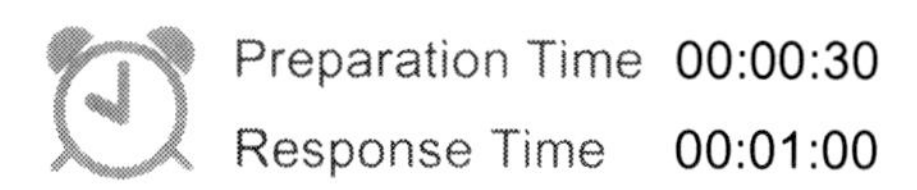

Use your 30 seconds of "Preparation Time" to organize your notes and prepare for your response.

Write your response on the lines below. Then **say your response aloud,** making sure that you can deliver your response within 1 minute.

Response

Model Answer

PASSAGE

Melodrama

A *melodrama* is a narrative that depicts characters and events that are exaggerated to appeal to audiences' emotions. Generally, characters in melodramas are extremely moral or immoral, and the plot is fast paced. Melodramas usually place these unrealistic characters and events in realistic settings, making the stories more relatable to audiences. Melodramas have existed since the 18th century, and the style has remained popular because melodramas allow audiences to escape from reality by engaging themselves in larger-than-life characters, emotions, and events.

Passage Notes

Main Idea: *melodrama = big chars., appeal to emo.*

- *fast paced, good vs. bad chars.*
- *realistic setting, provide aud. escape*

LECTURE

Popular culture often blends elements of melodrama with different genres. Now let's look at two examples of this blending: the 1939 American film Gone with the Wind *and the 2013 South Korean television show* My Love from the Star.

Adapted from the 1936 novel of the same name, Gone with the Wind *takes place in the southern United States during and after the American Civil War. The story follows Scarlett O'Hara, the daughter of a wealthy plantation owner, as she struggles to survive the destructive wake of the Civil War. The film uses melodramatic elements such as exaggerated characters, obsession, and a war-zone setting. Audiences and critics loved the mixture of melodrama and history, and the film was a huge box-office success.*

For a more recent example of melodrama, let's discuss the Korean show My Love from the Star. *The show follows a handsome alien who becomes stranded on Earth for centuries before falling in love with a beautiful actress. This show takes a science fiction plot — an alien being stranded on Earth — and adds many elements of melodrama: the plot centers on romance, and there are clear divisions between the good and evil characters. Mixing science fiction and melodrama has proven successful, as the show has become popular both in South Korea and abroad.*

Lecture Notes

Topic: *melodramas (Gone w/ Wind & My Love from Star)*

Example 1: *Gone w/ Wind (U.S.)*

- Details: *U.S. Civil War setting + romantic chars. = success*

Example 2: *My Love from Star (S. Korea)*

- Details: *sci-fi plot + melodrama (good/evil, romance) = success*

Prompt

Using details and examples from both the passage and the lecture, describe some qualities of melodramas and explain how they are used in film and television

Response

According to the passage, a melodrama is a story that places simplified characters and a good versus evil conflict in a realistic setting. The lecture talks about how melodramatic elements are often combined with other popular genres by giving two examples. First, the lecture discusses the American movie *Gone with the Wind*. The movie is set during the American Civil War, and it combines melodramatic characters and romance with the tragic consequences of the war. Additionally, the lecture talks about the South Korean television show *My Love from the Star*, a science fiction story that uses melodramatic romance and a good versus evil conflict. In it, a space alien falls in love with a human.

TASK 5

CONVERSATION

M: *Hey, Laura. Are you going to study tonight for your final in Professor Seldon's class?*

F: *Well, Professor Seldon is leading a review session tonight to prepare us for the final, but I won't be able to go. I'm worried, too; his finals are supposed to be really hard.*

M: *Why won't you be able to go to the review session?*

F: *I have to work at that time.*

M: *Can't you just ask for the night off? I'm sure someone will be able to cover your shift at the restaurant.*

F: *I don't think my manager will let me. I had to take a day off last week for another review session, and he didn't really seem happy about that. But I guess I could always ask.*

M: *And if that doesn't work, maybe you can organize a study group after the review session. That way you can study with other students, and they can tell you what Professor Seldon discussed during the final review.*

F: *Hmmm, I hadn't thought of that. It sounds like a good idea, as long as I can convince some people to show up for a study session.*

M: *I'm sure you can convince at least a few of your classmates to study with you. Anyway, it can't hurt to try.*

M: *Male Student* / **F:** *Female Student*

Conversation Notes

Speaker's problem: ______________________

- Solution 1: ______________________
- Solution 2: ______________________

Prompt

Briefly summarize the problem the speakers are discussing. Then state which of the two solutions from the conversation you would recommend. Explain the reasons for your recommendation.

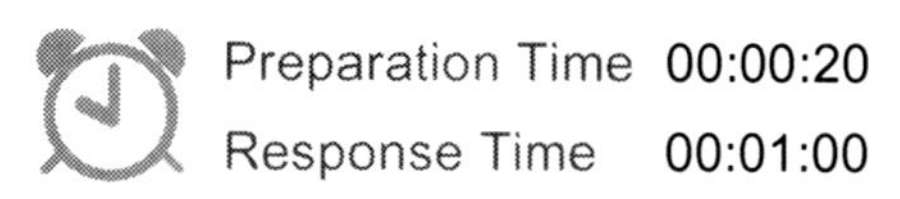

Use your 20 seconds of "Preparation Time" to organize your notes and prepare for your response.

Preparation Notes

Preferred solution: ____________________

- Reason 1: ____________________
- Reason 2: ____________________

Write your response on the lines below. Then **say your response aloud**, making sure that you can deliver your response within 1 minute.

Response

Model Answer

CONVERSATION

M: *Hey, Laura. Are you going to study tonight for your final in Professor Seldon's class?*

F: *Well, Professor Seldon is leading a review session tonight to prepare us for the final, but I won't be able to go. I'm worried, too; his finals are supposed to be really hard.*

M: *Why won't you be able to go to the review session?*

F: *I have to work at that time.*

M: *Can't you just ask for the night off? I'm sure someone will be able to cover your shift at the restaurant.*

F: *I don't think my manager will let me. I had to take a day off last week for another review session, and he didn't really seem happy about that. But I guess I could always ask.*

M: *And if that doesn't work, maybe you can organize a study group after the review session. That way you can study with other students, and they can tell you what Professor Seldon discussed during the final review.*

F: *Hmmm, I hadn't thought of that. It sounds like a good idea, as long as I can convince some people to show up for a study session.*

M: *I'm sure you can convince at least a few of your classmates to study with you. Anyway, it can't hurt to try.*

M: *Male Student* / **F:** *Female Student*

Conversation Notes

Speaker's problem: *woman → miss study sess. for final*

- Solution 1: *take night off from work*
- Solution 2: *hold own study group*

Prompt

Briefly summarize the problem the speakers are discussing. Then state which of the two solutions from the conversation you would recommend. Explain the reasons for your recommendation.

Preparation Notes

Preferred solution: *sol. 2*

- Reason 1: *no risk angering boss*
- Reason 2: *learn from other students*

Response

The issue discussed in the conversation is that the woman has a scheduling conflict between her job and a study session for her final exam. Of the two solutions proposed by the man, I think the woman should organize her own study session after she gets off work. One reason that this solution will work is that she won't have to risk angering her boss by asking for more time off. Moreover, if she invites some students who attended the first review session, she can find out what the professor talked about. Therefore, she can make sure she knows everything she needs to for the final exam.

LECTURE

Dragons in Mythology

Beliefs about dragons — mythical serpent- or reptile-like creatures — have developed in many cultures at different points in history. Historians suspect that the dragons depicted in legends were often based on ancient peoples' encounters with large reptiles, such as snakes and crocodiles. Accordingly, many ancient cultures believed that dragons inhabited rivers or caves. Despite some similarities, representations of dragons in European myths and legends differ greatly from those in East Asian traditions.

The dragons in European tales are usually the large, winged opponents of great heroes or gods. In ancient Greek mythology, the hero Hercules defeated the Lernaean Hydra, a many-headed serpentine dragon that guarded the entrance to the Underworld. Centuries later, the Scandinavian peoples of Northern Europe told the story of Beowulf, a great hero and king whose last great act was to slay a fearsome, cave-dwelling dragon that threatened his kingdom.

But Chinese myths regard dragons much differently. As early as the 16th century BCE, the Chinese have revered the dragon as a symbol of longevity, wisdom, and power. Some Chinese dynasties even associated dragons with the emperor. Over the course of centuries, this positive image of dragons spread throughout East Asia. In fact, one ancient Vietnamese myth told how all Vietnamese people were the offspring of the union between a fairy and a dragon.

Lecture Notes

Main Idea: ______________________________

Subtopic 1: ______________________________

- Details: ______________________________

____

Subtopic 2: ______________________________

- Details: ______________________________

____

Prompt

Using examples from the lecture, explain some similarities and differences between the dragons created by different cultures.

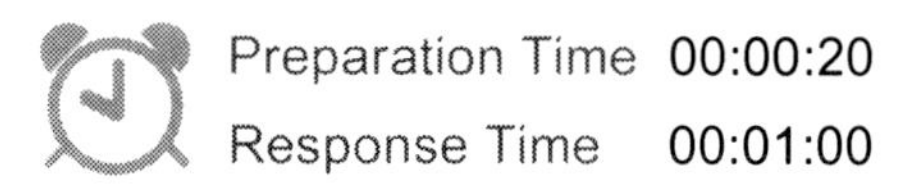

Use your 20 seconds of "Preparation Time" to organize your notes and prepare for your response.

Write your response on the lines below. Then **say your response aloud**, making sure that you can deliver your response within 1 minute.

Response

Model Answer

LECTURE

Dragons in Mythology

Beliefs about dragons — mythical serpent- or reptile-like creatures — have developed in many cultures at different points in history. Historians suspect that the dragons depicted in legends were often based on ancient peoples' encounters with large reptiles, such as snakes and crocodiles. Accordingly, many ancient cultures believed that dragons inhabited rivers or caves. Despite some similarities, representations of dragons in European myths and legends differ greatly from those in East Asian traditions.

The dragons in European tales are usually the large, winged opponents of great heroes or gods. In ancient Greek mythology, the hero Hercules defeated the Lernaean Hydra, a many-headed serpentine dragon that guarded the entrance to the Underworld. Centuries later, the Scandinavian peoples of Northern Europe told the story of Beowulf, a great hero and king whose last great act was to slay a fearsome, cave-dwelling dragon that threatened his kingdom.

But Chinese myths regard dragons much differently. As early as the 16th century BCE, the Chinese have revered the dragon as a symbol of longevity, wisdom, and power. Some Chinese dynasties even associated dragons with the emperor. Over the course of centuries, this positive image of dragons spread throughout East Asia. In fact, one ancient Vietnamese myth told how all Vietnamese people were the offspring of the union between a fairy and a dragon.

Lecture Notes

Main Idea: *dragons → Euro. & Asia have diff. myths (all from big reptiles)*

Subtopic 1: *Euro. dragons*

- Details: *wings, fire, evil*

  myths: Hercules vs. Hydra & Beowulf vs. dragon

Subtopic 2: *Asian dragons*

- Details: *China, 16th c. BCE, → dragons wise, powerful, royal*

  Viet. origin → dragon/fairy combo.

Prompt

Using examples from the lecture, explain some similarities and differences between the dragons created by different cultures.

Response

Dragons are depicted as large reptilian creatures that live in caves or rivers. According to the lecture, sightings of big reptiles such as snakes probably inspired myths about dragons in many cultures. European dragons are often the evil foes of great heroes. For example, in Greek mythology, the hero Hercules had to defeat the Hydra, a dragon with many heads. And in Northern European myths, the hero Beowulf killed a dragon to save his kingdom. However, Chinese mythical dragons are usually associated with wisdom, power, and royalty, not evil. This positive view of dragons spread to other parts of Asia. Ancient Vietnamese people even believed that they were descended from a fairy and a dragon.

TASK 1

Prompt

What was your favorite childhood activity? Describe this activity and explain why it was important to you. Use specific reasons and details to support your answer.

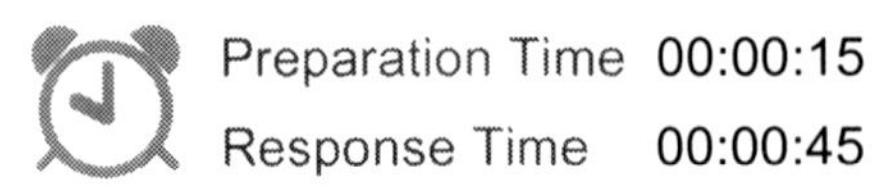

Notes

Opinion: ______________________________

- ______________________________
- ______________________________

Response

____

____

____

____

____

____

____

____

____

____

Prompt

When traveling, some people like to arrive at their final destination as quickly as possible; other people prefer to take their time and enjoy the journey. Which way of traveling do you prefer and why? Use specific reasons and example to support your answer.

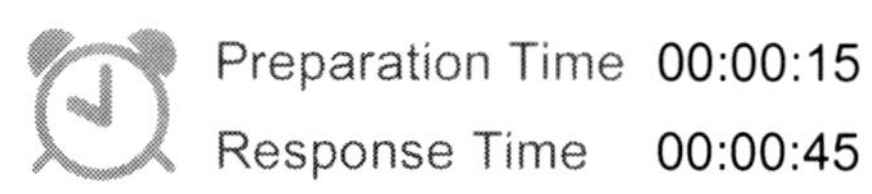

Notes

Preference: ______________________________

- ______________________________
- ______________________________

Response

____

____

____

____

____

____

____

____

____

____

TASK 1

Model Answer

Prompt

What was your favorite childhood activity? Describe this activity and explain why it was important to you. Use specific reasons and details to support your answer.

Notes

Opinion: *drawing*

- *expand my imagination*
- *can always get better*

Response

When I was a child, my favorite activity was drawing. One reason that I enjoyed drawing so much was that it allowed me to let my imagination run wild. Sometimes when I would read about a mythical creature, I'd try to imagine what it looked like so that I could draw it later. In fact, my childhood love of imagining and drawing has inspired me to pursue creative writing at a university. Another reason that I enjoyed drawing was that it was something that I could always get better at. No matter how good I thought one of my drawings was, I was always able to find some way to make it just a little bit better, so drawing was a fun, never-ending project.

Model Answer

Prompt

When traveling, some people like to arrive at their final destination as quickly as possible; other people prefer to take their time and enjoy the journey. Which way of traveling do you prefer and why? Use specific reasons and example to support your answer.

Notes

Preference: *enjoy the journey*

- *don't like being rushed*
- *enjoy surprises, no scheduling*

Response

When I travel, I prefer to take my time traveling from one place to another for a couple of reasons. First, I don't like being rushed, so trying to travel from point "A" to point "B" as quickly as possible has always made me feel stressed and anxious. I enjoy spending as much time traveling as being at my destination because doing so allows me to stop and enjoy scenery. Additionally, I don't like planning things out in advance, so when I travel, I enjoy being surprised and letting myself get sidetracked. Doing so lets me have many unique, unexpected experiences.

UNIVERSITY ANNOUNCEMENT

University Schedule Changes

The university is proposing to change its class meeting times and days. Currently, most classes meet Monday through Friday for 40 minutes each period. The university would like to change this schedule, offering some of these classes on Monday, Wednesday, and Friday for 50-minute periods; some on Tuesday and Thursday for 90-minute periods; and some on single weekdays for 3-hour periods. By changing classes to these times, the university will be able to offer more classes, and students will have more time to study between classes.

Announcement Notes

Proposal: ____________________

- ____________________
- ____________________

CONVERSATION

F: *I'm actually pretty excited about this change in class meeting time.*

M: *Really? I'm not so sure about it myself.*

F: *Well, think about it: meeting for class only two or three days a week will make it so much easier to balance your work schedule with your class times. And having a day to study between classes will be great, too.*

M: *Huh, I guess I hadn't thought about it that way. It'll be nice to have a more flexible school schedule.*

F: *Exactly! And I think classes will be less crowded with the new meeting times. I mean, people will sign up for the same class on different days, so we can finally sit closer to the front of the class and hear our professor in those huge introductory lecture halls.*

M: *That's actually a really good point. If one class is offered on several different days, it's bound to be less crowded than now.*

F: *Female Student* / **M:** *Male Student*

Conversation Notes

Speaker's opinion: ____________________

- ____________________
- ____________________

Prompt

The woman expresses her opinion about the plan described in the announcement. Briefly summarize the plan. Then state her opinion about the plan and explain the reasons she gives for holding that opinion.

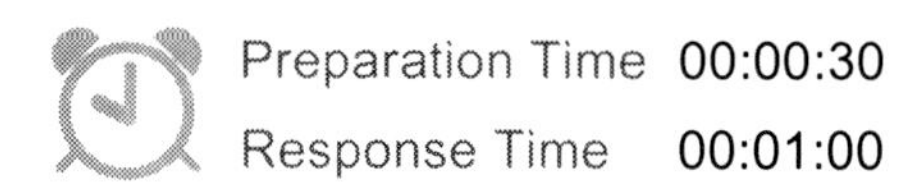

Use your 30 seconds of "Preparation Time" to organize your notes and prepare for your response.

Write your response on the lines below. Then **say your response aloud,** making sure that you can deliver your response within 1 minute.

Response

Model Answer

UNIVERSITY ANNOUNCEMENT

University Schedule Changes

The university is proposing to change its class meeting times and days. Currently, most classes meet Monday through Friday for 40 minutes each period. The university would like to change this schedule, offering some of these classes on Monday, Wednesday, and Friday for 50-minute periods; some on Tuesday and Thursday for 90-minute periods; and some on single weekdays for 3-hour periods. By changing classes to these times, the university will be able to offer more classes, and students will have more time to study between classes.

Announcement Notes

Proposal: *change class meeting times (M.W.F. & T.Th. classes)*

- *offer ↑ classes*
- *↑ study time b/w classes*

CONVERSATION

F: *I'm actually pretty excited about this change in class meeting time.*

M: *Really? I'm not so sure about it myself.*

F: *Well, think about it: meeting for class only two or three days a week will make it so much easier to balance your work schedule with your class times. And having a day to study between classes will be great, too.*

M: *Huh, I guess I hadn't thought about it that way. It'll be nice to have a more flexible school schedule.*

F: *Exactly! And I think classes will be less crowded with the new meeting times. I mean, people will sign up for the same class on different days, so we can finally sit closer to the front of the class and hear our professor in those huge introductory lecture halls.*

M: *That's actually a really good point. If one class is offered on several different days, it's bound to be less crowded than now.*

F: Female Student / **M:** Male Student

Conversation Notes

Speaker's opinion: *man supports*

- *easier to balance work/school scheds., ↑ study time*
- *classes ↓ crowded → better seats*

Prompt

The woman expresses her opinion about the plan described in the announcement. Briefly summarize the plan. Then state her opinion about the plan and explain the reasons she gives for holding that opinion.

Response

The university plans to change its class scheduling from holding each class every weekday to holding each class on every other weekday. Thus, some classes will be held on Mondays, Wednesdays, and Fridays, while others will be on Tuesdays and Thursdays. The female speaker supports this proposal for a couple of reasons. First, she thinks that the schedule change will make it easier for students to manage their academic and work schedules. And she also thinks that the alternating class days will give students more time to study between each class session. Second, the female student believes that the school will be able to offer more classes with this new schedule, reducing the number of students in each class and making it easier to learn.

PASSAGE

Synesthesia

Synesthesia is a neurological condition in which the stimulation of one sense causes automatic stimulation of another sense. For instance, the most common form, called *grapheme-color synesthesia*, causes a person to perceive all letters and numbers as colored. Those who experience synesthesia are called *synesthetes*. Synesthesia can occur between any two senses, and in rare cases it has affected more than two. Most synesthetes claim that they benefit from their condition, as it often improves memory and facilitates creativity.

Passage Notes

Main Idea: ______________________________

- ______________________________
- ______________________________

LECTURE

Now that you have an idea of what synesthesia is, let's look at two individuals who had synesthesia so we can better understand how this condition affects perception.

Twentieth-century Russian author Vladimir Nabokov possessed grapheme-color synesthesia. When he was asked what colors his initials were, he responded that the "V" is a pale-pink color while the "N" is yellowish-gray. Interestingly, the multilingual author perceived the coloration of the same letters differently depending on the language. For instance, Nabokov associated the pronunciation of the letter "a" in English with a different color than that of an "a" in French.

Solomon Shereshevsky was a Russian man who lived during the 19th and 20th centuries. He possessed the only recorded case of fivefold synesthesia: any time one of his senses was stimulated, it triggered a reaction in all of his other senses. As a result, Shereshevsky possessed an incredible memory, and he was able to memorize long mathematical formulas, speeches, and even poems in foreign languages. But he was also very susceptible to sensory overload.

Lecture Notes

Topic: ______________________________

Example 1: ______________________________

- Details: ______________________________

Example 2: ______________________________

- Details: ______________________________

Prompt

Using details and examples from both the passage and the lecture, explain how synesthesia can alter a person's perceptions of the world.

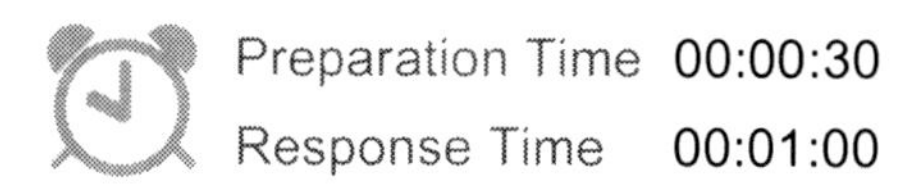

Use your 30 seconds of "Preparation Time" to organize your notes and prepare for your response.

Write your response on the lines below. Then **say your response aloud,** making sure that you can deliver your response within 1 minute.

Response

Model Answer

PASSAGE

Synesthesia

Synesthesia is a neurological condition in which the stimulation of one sense causes automatic stimulation of another sense. For instance, the most common form, called *grapheme-color synesthesia*, causes a person to perceive all letters and numbers as colored. Those who experience synesthesia are called *synesthetes*. Synesthesia can occur between any two senses, and in rare cases it has affected more than two. Most synesthetes claim that they benefit from their condition, as it often improves memory and facilitates creativity.

Passage Notes

Main Idea: *synesthesia = 1 sense → 1+ other sense*

- *graph-color syn. = letters/#s → colored*
- *syn. ↑ memory & creativity*

LECTURE

Now that you have an idea of what synesthesia is, let's look at two individuals who had synesthesia so we can better understand how this condition affects perception.

Solomon Shereshevsky was a Russian man who lived during the 19th and 20th centuries. He possessed the only recorded case of fivefold synesthesia: any time one of his senses was stimulated, it triggered a reaction in all of his other senses. As a result, Shereshevsky possessed an incredible memory, and he was able to memorize long mathematical formulas, speeches, and even poems in foreign languages. But he was also very susceptible to sensory overload.

Twentieth-century Russian author Vladimir Nabokov possessed grapheme-color synesthesia. When he was asked what colors his initials were, he responded that the "V" is a pale-pink color while the "N" is yellowish-gray. Interestingly, the multilingual author perceived the coloration of the same letters differently depending on the language. For instance, Nabokov associated the pronunciation of the letter "a" in English with a different color than that of an "a" in French.

Lecture Notes

Topic: *S. Shereshevsky (SS) & V. Nabokov (VN)*

Example 1: *SS*

- Details: *1 sense → all senses; incredible memory, overloaded*

Example 2: *VN*

- Details: *author, graph-color syn.; letter/# color changed based on lang.*

Prompt

Using details and examples from both the passage and the lecture, explain how synesthesia can alter a person's perceptions of the world.

Response

The passage talks about a condition called synesthesia that causes a sensation to trigger one or more other sensations in the body. For example, the author Vladimir Nabokov had a relatively common form of synesthesia called grapheme-color synesthesia, which caused him to see all numbers and letters as colored. He would even see the same letter as colored differently if it was used in a different language. Most people with synesthesia claim that it helps them remember things better and boosts their creativity. One man, named Solomon Shereshevsky, had a type of synesthesia where activating one of his senses would trigger every other sense at once. According to the lecture, the condition gave him an incredible memory, but he'd sometimes become overwhelmed.

CONVERSATION

F: *What's up, Andrew? You look pretty upset.*

M: *Well, I'm pretty sure the teaching assistant who grades all of the assignments in my literature class is intentionally giving me bad grades.*

F: *Wow! Really? Why would your TA pick on you?*

M: *I think it's because I disagreed with his interpretation of the reading when I talked to him after class a couple of weeks ago. Before that, he loved my writing, but now he gives me terrible grades with no feedback.*

F: *That's totally unacceptable.*

M: *Yeah, but I don't know what to do about it.*

F: *Well, you could always talk to your professor. He should know if one of his TAs is being unfair.*

M: *The only problem is that the professor really likes this TA. I'm afraid the professor will side with the TA and start disliking me too. Then my grade will really suffer.*

F: *You could also drop the class and take it next semester. At least then there will be a different TA for the class.*

M: *That's true, but then all my hard work in the class will be wasted. Thanks for your advice, though. I'll definitely consider those options.*

F: *Female Student* / **M:** *Male Student*

Conversation Notes

Speaker's problem: ______________________________

- Solution 1: ______________________________
- Solution 2: ______________________________

Prompt

Briefly summarize the problem the speakers are discussing. Then state which of the two solutions from the conversation you would recommend. Explain the reasons for your recommendation.

Preparation Time 00:00:20
Response Time 00:01:00

Use your 20 seconds of "Preparation Time" to organize your notes and prepare for your response.

Preparation Notes

Preferred solution: ______________________________

- Reason 1: ______________________________
- Reason 2: ______________________________

Write your response on the lines below. Then **say your response aloud,** making sure that you can deliver your response within 1 minute.

Response

____

____

____

____

____

____

____

____

____

____

Model Answer

CONVERSATION

F: *What's up, Andrew? You look pretty upset.*

M: *Well, I'm pretty sure the teaching assistant who grades all of the assignments in my literature class is intentionally giving me bad grades.*

F: *Wow! Really? Why would your TA pick on you?*

M: *I think it's because I disagreed with his interpretation of the reading when I talked to him after class a couple of weeks ago. Before that, he loved my writing, but now he gives me terrible grades with no feedback.*

F: *That's totally unacceptable.*

M: *Yeah, but I don't know what to do about it.*

F: *Well, you could always talk to your professor. He should know if one of his TAs is being unfair.*

M: *The only problem is that the professor really likes this TA. I'm afraid the professor will side with the TA and start disliking me too. Then my grade will really suffer.*

F: *You could also drop the class and take it next semester. At least then there will be a different TA for the class.*

M: *That's true, but then all my hard work in the class will be wasted. Thanks for your advice, though. I'll definitely consider those options.*

F: Female Student / **M:** Male Student

Conversation Notes

Speaker's problem: *man → TA giving bad grades on purpose*

- Solution 1: *talk to prof.*
- Solution 2: *drop class, take next semester*

Prompt

Briefly summarize the problem the speakers are discussing. Then state which of the two solutions from the conversation you would recommend. Explain the reasons for your recommendation.

Preparation Notes

Preferred solution: *sol. 1*

- Reason 1: *can always drop class after discussing w/ prof.*
- Reason 2: *prof. should know abt. this issue*

Response

The issue being discussed by the two students is that a teaching assistant for the man's class may be intentionally giving him bad grades. Of the two solutions proposed by the woman, I think that Andrew should choose to talk to his professor about the issue. For one, if the professor sides with the teaching assistant, as Andrew fears, he could still drop the class after that and take a different literature class next semester. After all, who would want to take a class from a professor who refuses to listen to reason? Additionally, the professor needs to be made aware that one of his teaching assistants is being incredibly unfair. If this TA's not confronted about his unfair grading, then he may continue to do it to other students in the future.

LECTURE

Gymnosperms and Angiosperms

At one point, plant life on Earth was dominated by mosses and ferns, which reproduce by releasing spores that grow into plants in damp environments. But about 300 million years ago, plants began developing a new system for reproduction: seeds. Today, two groups of seed-producing plants dominate land habitats.

The first group of plants to reproduce by spreading seeds are called gymnosperms, a term that means "naked seed" in Greek. Gymnosperms include pine trees, fir trees, and cycads, all of which produce clusters of uncovered seeds in cones. Gymnosperms reproduce by releasing pollen, which is carried by the wind to other gymnosperms of the same species. This pollen then fertilizes the gymnosperms' exposed seeds. Once the pollinated seeds fall to the ground, they can sprout into a new gymnosperm.

About 150 million years after the first gymnosperms appeared, the development of angiosperms, which are usually called flowering plants, gave rise to a more effective form of pollination. The pollination of flowering plants depends on animals. The flower portion of an angiosperm uses sugary nectar to lure insects, birds, and mammals, which unwittingly collect the angiosperm's pollen on their bodies as they feed of the flower's nectar. Then, when the animal feeds on the next nectary flower, the animal deposits the pollen from the previous flower, leading to fertilization. Fertilized angiosperms then form seeds encased in a fruit. Animals eat the fruit and spread the seeds in the droppings. Today, there are about 280,000 known species of angiosperm, and only about 1,000 know gymnosperm species.

Lecture Notes

Main Idea: ______________________________

Subtopic 1: ______________________________

- Details: ______________________________

____

Subtopic 2: ______________________________

- Details: ______________________________

____

Prompt

Using points and details from he lecture, explain the different reproductive processes of gymnosperms and angiosperms.

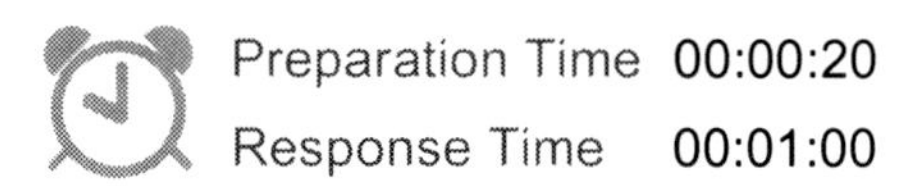

Use your 20 seconds of "Preparation Time" to organize your notes and prepare for your response.

Write your response on the lines below. Then **say your response aloud**, making sure that you can deliver your response within 1 minute.

Response

Model Answer

LECTURE

Gymnosperms and Angiosperms

At one point, plant life on Earth was dominated by mosses and ferns, which reproduce by releasing spores that grow into plants in damp environments. But about 300 million years ago, plants began developing a new system for reproduction: seeds. Today, two groups of seed-producing plants dominate land habitats.

The first group of plants to reproduce by spreading seeds are called gymnosperms, a term that means "naked seed" in Greek. Gymnosperms include pine trees, fir trees, and cycads, all of which produce clusters of uncovered seeds in cones. Gymnosperms reproduce by releasing pollen, which is carried by the wind to other gymnosperms of the same species. This pollen then fertilizes the gymnosperms' exposed seeds. Once the pollinated seeds fall to the ground, they can sprout into a new gymnosperm.

About 150 million years after the first gymnosperms appeared, the development of angiosperms, which are usually called flowering plants, gave rise to a more effective form of pollination. The pollination of flowering plants depends on animals. The flower portion of an angiosperm uses sugary nectar to lure insects, birds, and mammals, which unwittingly collect the angiosperm's pollen on their bodies as they feed of the flower's nectar. Then, when the animal feeds on the next nectary flower, the animal deposits the pollen from the previous flower, leading to fertilization. Fertilized angiosperms then form seeds encased in a fruit. Animals eat the fruit and spread the seeds in the droppings. Today, there are about 280,000 known species of angiosperm, and only about 1,000 know gymnosperm species.

Lecture Notes

Main Idea: *seed-producing plants*

Subtopic 1: *gymnosperm reproduction (300 mil. yrs. ago)*

- Details: *pines, firs, cycads; pollen carried by wind to cone seeds, seeds fall to ground & grow*

Subtopic 2: *angiosperm reproduction (150 mil. yrs. ago)*

- Details: *flower plants; flowers lure animals, animals carry pollen from plant to plant, seeds in fruit, animals spread seeds*

Prompt

Using points and details from he lecture, explain the different reproductive processes of gymnosperms and angiosperms.

 **Response**

The lecture discusses the reproductive processes of angiosperms and gymnosperms. The first gymnosperms developed about 300 million years ago. They produce exposed seeds in cones. Wind carries pollen from one gymnosperm to another, fertilizing the seeds. The fertilized seeds fall to the ground and grow into a new plant. Angiosperms, which appeared 150 million years after gymnosperms, use nectar to attract animals. Animals get an angiosperm's pollen on them when they drink its nectar, spreading the pollen from plant to plant. Once an angiosperm is pollinated, it creates a fruit with seeds. Animals eat the fruit, and spread the seeds in their droppings. The seeds then grow into new plants.

TASK 1

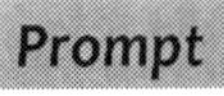

Describe a past action you have taken of which you are very proud. Explain why you are proud of this action. Use specific reasons and examples to support your answer.

Preparation Time 00:00:15
Response Time 00:00:45

Notes

Opinion: ______________________________

- ______________________________
- ______________________________

Response

____

____

____

____

____

____

____

____

____

____

Prompt

Some people spend their entire lives in one place. Others move a number of times throughout their lives, looking for a better job, house, community, or climate. Which do you prefer: staying in one place or moving in search of another place? Use specific reasons and details to support your answer.

Preparation Time 00:00:15
Response Time 00:00:45

Notes

Preference: ____________________

- ____________________
- ____________________

Response

____

____

____

____

____

____

____

____

____

____

Model Answer

Prompt

Describe a past action you have taken of which you are very proud. Explain why you are proud of this action. Use specific reasons and examples to support your answer.

Notes

Opinion: *completed a triathlon*

- *required a lot of training*
- *beat my goal time*

Response

One accomplishment that I am proud of is completing a triathlon when I was 16 years old. One reason I am proud of this accomplishment is that I had to practice swimming, biking, and running for many months to properly prepare for the triathlon. All that training got me in good shape for the event and helped me lose more than 10 pounds. Additionally, I'm proud of myself for completing the triathlon because I was able to finish before I thought I would. Before the triathlon, I ambitiously set a goal time that I thought I could never reach, but I was able to finish five minutes before my goal.

Model Answer

Prompt

Some people spend their entire lives in one place. Others move a number of times throughout their lives, looking for a better job, house, community, or climate. Which do you prefer: staying in one place or moving in search of another place? Use specific reasons and details to support your answer.

Notes

Preference: *stay in one place*

- *able to raise fam.*
- *steadier job/lifestyle*

Response

If I had to choose between living in one place and moving often, I'd choose to live in one place for a couple of reasons. First, I have always dreamed of raising a big family someday, and I believe it's best to raise a family in one location. That way, my children can have a sense of stability, and they can have the same friends as they grow up. Moreover, I believe that living in one place would allow me to maintain a steady job and develop a routine in my life, two things that I find very important . If I had to move constantly, I think I'd become too stressed out by all the changes I'd have to endure.

UNIVERSITY ANNOUNCEMENT

University President to Institute New Dorm Rules

Due to a number of recent incidents in the dorms, the university has decided to introduce new rules that will hopefully improve dorm conditions for all students. First, In order to prevent late-night noise and partying, there will be a new "lights out" curfew of 12:00 am during the week. Additionally, the cost of any damage to school property in the dorms will be distributed equally among all students in that dorm building. Hopefully, this last rule will motivate students to keep a watchful eye in case things get out of hand on their floors.

Announcement Notes

Proposal: ____________________

- ____________________
- ____________________

CONVERSATION

M: *Did you read this article in the school paper about the new dorm rules?*

F: *I did. I hope these rules will stop all the weeknight partying.*

M: *Maybe, but the university shouldn't be punishing everyone in the dorms! Only a few people party in the dorms during the week. The university needs to find and discipline those students, not make new rules for everyone!*

F: *Well, I guess that's true.*

M: *I mean, what's the deal with the 12 am "lights out" policy? I study almost every night until 2 am in my dorm. I don't think I'll be able to pass half of my classes if I have to go to bed at midnight every night.*

F: *I definitely agree with you there. I guess we'll have to study in the library if we want to get any work done after 12 am.*

M: *And do you know what bugs me the most? The university is forcing the entire floor of a dorm to pay for any damages. I mean, I'm not gonna waste my time policing everyone else in my dorm; I'm here to learn, not to act as campus security for fear of having to pay for others' messes.*

F: *Yeah, that is a ridiculous rule. Maybe we should talk to the administration about this.*

Conversation Notes

Speaker's opinion: ____________________

- ____________________
- ____________________

Prompt

The male student expresses his opinion of the new dorm rules in the article. State his opinion and the reasons he gives for holding that opinion.

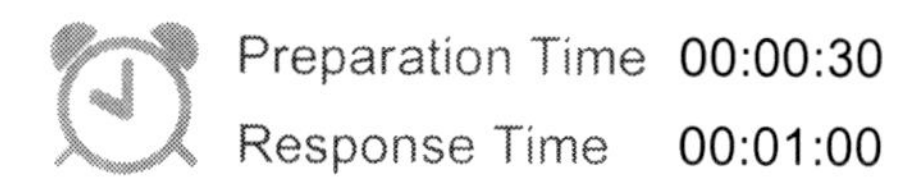

Use your 30 seconds of "Preparation Time" to organize your notes and prepare for your response.

Write your response on the lines below. Then **say your response aloud,** making sure that you can deliver your response within 1 minute.

Response

Model Answer

UNIVERSITY ANNOUNCEMENT

University President to Institute New Dorm Rules

Due to a number of recent incidents in the dorms, the university has decided to introduce new rules that will hopefully improve dorm conditions for all students. First, In order to prevent late-night noise and partying, there will be a new "lights out" curfew of 12:00 am during the week. Additionally, the cost of any damage to school property in the dorms will be distributed equally among all students in that dorm building. Hopefully, this last rule will motivate students to keep a watchful eye in case things get out of hand on their floors.

Announcement Notes

Proposal: *new dorm rules to prevent partying*

- *curfew → 12 am*
- *all students have to pay for dorm damage*

CONVERSATION

M: *Did you read this article in the school paper about the new dorm rules?*

F: *I did. I hope these rules will stop all the weeknight partying.*

M: *Maybe, but the university shouldn't be punishing everyone in the dorms! Only a few people party in the dorms during the week. The university needs to find and discipline those students, not make new rules for everyone!*

F: *Well, I guess that's true.*

M: *I mean, what's the deal with the 12 am "lights out" policy? I study almost every night until 2 am in my dorm. I don't think I'll be able to pass half of my classes if I have to go to bed at midnight every night.*

F: *I definitely agree with you there. I guess we'll have to study in the library if we want to get any work done after 12 am.*

M: *And do you know what bugs me the most? The university is forcing the entire floor of a dorm to pay for any damages. I mean, I'm not gonna waste my time policing everyone else in my dorm; I'm here to learn, not to act as campus security for fear of having to pay for others' messes.*

F: *Yeah, that is a ridiculous rule. Maybe we should talk to the administration about this.*

Conversation Notes

Speaker's opinion: *man opposes*

- *curfew → not enough time to study*
- *$ for damage → students shouldn't have to police/pay for others*

Prompt

The male student expresses his opinion of the new dorm rules in the article. State his opinion and the reasons he gives for holding that opinion.

Response

The university is introducing new dormitory rules to stop students from partying and making too much noise. The university will require students to turn off their lights at midnight during the week, and it'll make all students in a dorm pay for any damages to the dorm. The man opposes these new rules. First, he claims that the new curfew of 12 am won't give him enough time to study because he usually studies in his dorm until 2 am. Second, he opposes the rule that requires all students to pay for any damages to the dorms because he feels that it's unfair he has to pay for the mistakes of others. Moreover, he opposes this rule because he doesn't feel like he should have to waste his time policing the dorms to make sure no one's damaging anything.

PASSAGE

Brown v. Board of Education

Even well into the 20th century, much of America remained highly *segregated*, or socially separated based on ethnicity. Especially in the southern states, laws forbade black people from using the same public facilities as white people. Many considered such laws fair as long as the racially separated facilities were of equal quality. However, the 1954 Supreme Court case *Brown v. Board of Education* challenged the legality of "separate but equal" facilities. In a historic, unanimous decision, the Supreme Court justices ruled that separating students because of their race had negative psychological effects that harmed students' learning, so separate facilities were inherently unequal.

Passage Notes

Main Idea: ____________________

- ____________________
- ____________________

LECTURE

Now that you have some background knowledge on this significant Supreme Court decision, let's look at some of its immediate and long term effects.

For instance, in 1958 and 1959, policies collectively referred to as Massive Resistance developed in Virginia. These policies ensured that Virginia schools were shut down before becoming desegregated. In fact, the policies gained enough strength to have an entire school system temporarily shut down. But state and federal judges declared these policies unconstitutional, and the desegregation of schools continued.

Moreover, by overturning laws that upheld segregation, Brown v. Board of Education *represented a huge step forward for the American Civil Rights Movement. Essentially, the case forced many to recognize that true racial equality can only be achieved through integration, not segregation. The desegregation of public schools fueled a political and social push for an end to all forms of discrimination. So for many, the passing of the Civil Rights Act of 1965, which outlawed racial and religious discrimination, marked a high point in the process begun by* Brown v. Board of Education.

Lecture Notes

Topic: ____________________

Example 1: ____________________

- Details: ____________________

Example 2: ____________________

- Details: ____________________

Prompt

Using details and examples from both the passage and the lecture, describe some of the immediate and long-term effects of the *Brown v. Board of Education* Supreme Court decision.

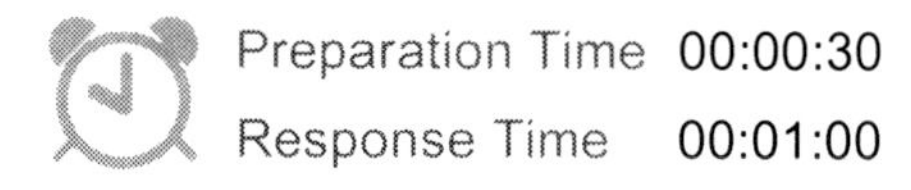

Use your 30 seconds of "Preparation Time" to organize your notes and prepare for your response.

Write your response on the lines below. Then **say your response aloud,** making sure that you can deliver your response within 1 minute.

Response

Model Answer

PASSAGE

Brown v. Board of Education

Even well into the 20th century, much of America remained highly *segregated*, or socially separated based on ethnicity. Especially in the southern states, laws forbade black people from using the same public facilities as white people. Many considered such laws fair as long as the racially separated facilities were of equal quality. However, the 1954 Supreme Court case *Brown v. Board of Education* challenged the legality of "separate but equal" facilities. In a historic, unanimous decision, the Supreme Court Justices ruled that separating students because of their race had negative psychological effects that harmed students' learning, so separate facilities were by nature unequal.

Passage Notes

Main Idea: *Brown v. Board supreme court case (1954) → abt. segregation*

- *ended "separate but equal" places*
- *these places bad for psych., so they aren't equal*

LECTURE

Now that you have some background knowledge on this significant Supreme Court decision, let's look at some of its immediate and long term effects.

For instance, in 1958 and 1959, policies collectively referred to as Massive Resistance developed in Virginia. These policies ensured that Virginia schools were shut down before becoming desegregated. In fact, the policies gained enough strength to have an entire school system temporarily shut down. But state and federal judges declared these policies unconstitutional, and the desegregation of schools continued.

Moreover, by overturning laws that upheld segregation, Brown v. Board of Education *represented a huge step forward for the American Civil Rights Movement. Essentially, the case forced many to recognize that true racial equality can only be achieved through integration, not segregation. The desegregation of public schools fueled a political and social push for an end to all forms of discrimination. So for many, the passing of the Civil Rights Act of 1965, which outlawed racial and religious discrimination, marked a high point in the process begun by* Brown v. Board of Education.

Lecture Notes

Topic: *effects of Brown v. Board*

Example 1: *resistance*

- Details: *Massive Resist. (VA) shut down schools before deseg., deemed unconstitutional*

Example 2: *equality*

- Details: *helped end all seg. (Civil Rights Act 1965)*

Prompt

Using details and examples from both the passage and the lecture, describe some of the immediate and long-term effects of the *Brown v. Board of Education* Supreme Court decision.

Response

The passage discusses the 1954 U.S. Supreme Court case of Brown vs. Board, which outlawed "separate but equal" public spaces. In other words, the case made it so black people could use the same facilities as white people. Some people, especially in the South, opposed this decision. For example, some people in Virginia started the Massive Resistance in 1958 and 1959, which tried to pass laws that shut down schools rather than desegregate them. But the policies were quickly declared unconstitutional by American judges, and massive Resistance failed. The Brown v. Board case also encouraged an end to all segregation. The success of the case led to the Civil Rights Act of 1965, which made any form of discrimination illegal.

TASK 5

CONVERSATION

A: *Hello. Is there something I can help you with? You look upset.*

MS: *Actually, there is. I'm a freshman this year, and I'm having a lot of trouble making friends. I don't think of myself as antisocial or anything; I just can't seem to find people who share my interests.*

A: *I'm sorry to hear that. Don't worry, a lot of students have trouble making friends in such a new environment. Do you spend a lot of time with your roommate? Maybe he has a lot in common with you.*

MS: *Well, I live in a single, so I don't really have anyone to talk to in my dorm.*

A: *In that case, one solution to your feelings of loneliness could be moving into a double. Having a roommate will provide many chances for socializing. Who knows, maybe you guys will become great friends!*

MS: *I guess that could work. But I've never shared a room before; that's why I applied for a single this year. I'm worried I might not get along well with a roommate, and then I'll have even more problems than I do now.*

A: *That's a possibility, but you'll never know unless you try. Or you can always join one of the university's many intramural sports teams. They're not very competitive, but everyone agrees that they're a lot of fun. And team sports are a great way to meet and interact with new people.*

MS: *Well, I've never been very enthusiastic about team sports, but maybe that's a good idea. Thanks for the suggestions, you've been very helpful.*

A: *No problem, and I hope you can find friends on campus soon.*

A: *Advisor* / **MS:** *Male Student*

Conversation Notes

Speaker's problem: ______________________________

- Solution 1: ______________________________
- Solution 2: ______________________________

Prompt

Briefly summarize the problem the speakers are discussing. Then state which of the two solutions from the conversation you would recommend. Explain the reasons for your recommendation.

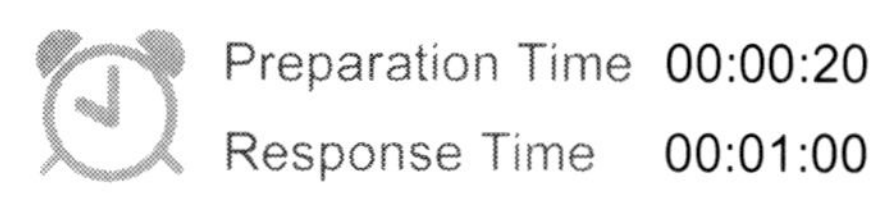

Use your 20 seconds of "Preparation Time" to organize your notes and prepare for your response.

Preparation Notes

Preferred solution: ______________________

- Reason 1: ______________________
- Reason 2: ______________________

Write your response on the lines below. Then **say your response aloud**, making sure that you can deliver your response within 1 minute.

Response

____

____

____

____

____

____

____

____

____

____

Model Answer

CONVERSATION

A: Hello. Is there something I can help you with? You look upset.

MS: Actually, there is. I'm a freshman this year, and I'm having a lot of trouble making friends. I don't think of myself as antisocial or anything; I just can't seem to find people who share my interests.

A: I'm sorry to hear that. Don't worry, a lot of students have trouble making friends in such a new environment. Do you spend a lot of time with your roommate? Maybe he has a lot in common with you.

MS: Well, I live in a single, so I don't really have anyone to talk to in my dorm.

A: In that case, one solution to your feelings of loneliness could be moving into a double. Having a roommate will provide many chances for socializing. Who knows, maybe you guys will become great friends!

MS: I guess that could work. But I've never shared a room before; that's why I applied for a single this year. I'm worried I might not get along well with a roommate, and then I'll have even more problems than I do now.

A: That's a possibility, but you'll never know unless you try. Or you can always join one of the university's many intramural sports teams. They're not very competitive, but everyone agrees that they're a lot of fun. And team sports are a great way to meet and interact with new people.

MS: Well, I've never been very enthusiastic about team sports, but maybe that's a good idea. Thanks for the suggestions, you've been very helpful.

A: No problem, and I hope you can find friends on campus soon.

A: Advisor / **MS:** Male Student

Conversation Notes

Speaker's problem: *student → trouble making friends*

- Solution 1: *move from single → double room (get roommate)*
- Solution 2: *join IM sports team*

Prompt

Briefly summarize the problem the speakers are discussing. Then state which of the two solutions from the conversation you would recommend. Explain the reasons for your recommendation.

Preparation Notes

Preferred solution: *sol. 2*

- Reason 1: *moving from single to double → can be risky*
- Reason 2: *sports → great way to bond w/ others*

Response

In the conversation, the student is telling the advisor that, as a freshman, he's having trouble making new friends. The advisor suggests that he either move from a single room to a double or join an intramural sports team. Of these two options, I think he should join the sports team. For one, moving from a single to a double could be quite risky. Although he may like his roommate, it's just as likely that the student wouldn't get along with his roommate, and that might make his friendship problems even worse. Additionally, I believe that sports can be a great way to bond with others. Even though the student says that he doesn't like sports very much, he can always join an intramural softball team, which may provide more opportunities for socializing than it does for competition.

LECTURE

Memory Retrieval

Today we'll talk about memory retrieval. But before we do so, we need to look briefly at how memories are made. Suppose that you're studying for a psychology test. When you read your textbook, you're encoding information; this means that you're converting words on the page into a memory that's stored in the brain. But a memory that's stored away is useless unless it can be retrieved, so now I'd like to discuss two types of memory retrieval that you might use on a test.

First, let's look at recognition. This is the process used by your brain during a multiple choice test. When you read the correct answer choice to a multiple-choice question, your brain recognizes that it has seen that information before. Thus, recognition is easier than other memory-retrieval processes because your brain only has to acknowledge that the information is familiar.

The other memory retrieval process I'd like to discuss is called recall, which is the process used during a written test. During recall, your brain must be able to access information without any external cues. That's why many students claim that written questions are more difficult than multiple choice ones: it's harder to recall information than it is to recognize something you've seen or heard before.

Lecture Notes

Main Idea: ______________________________

Subtopic 1: ______________________________

- Details: ______________________________

____

Subtopic 2: ______________________________

- Details: ______________________________

____

Prompt

Using points and details form the lecture, describe the two types of memory retrieval explained by the professor.

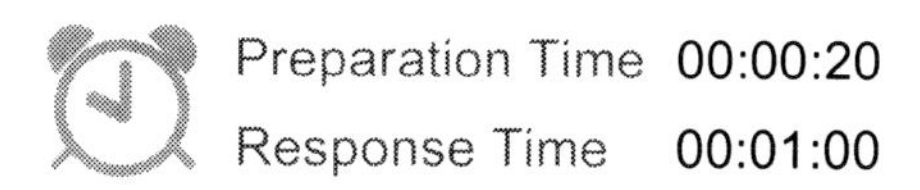

Use your 20 seconds of "Preparation Time" to organize your notes and prepare for your response.

Write your response on the lines below. Then **say your response aloud**, making sure that you can deliver your response within 1 minute.

Response

Model Answer

LECTURE

Memory Retrieval

Today we'll talk about memory retrieval. But before we do so, we need to look briefly at how memories are made. Suppose that you're studying for a psychology test. When you read your textbook, you're encoding information; this means that you're converting words on the page into a memory that's stored in the brain. But a memory that's stored away is useless unless it can be retrieved, so now I'd like to discuss two types of memory retrieval that you might use on a test.

First, let's look at recognition. This is the process used by your brain during a multiple choice test. When you read the correct answer choice to a multiple-choice question, your brain recognizes that it has seen that information before. Thus, recognition is easier than other memory-retrieval processes because your brain only has to acknowledge that the information is familiar.

The other memory retrieval process I'd like to discuss is called recall, which is the process used during a written test. During recall, your brain must be able to access information without any external cues. That's why many students claim that written questions are more difficult than multiple choice ones: it's harder to recall information than it is to recognize something you've seen or heard before.

Lecture Notes

Main Idea: *memory retrieval (accessing stored memories)*

Subtopic 1: *recognition*

- Details: *recover info. from memory by seeing it*

  used in MC test

Subtopic 2: *recall*

- Details: *recover info. from memory w/o seeing it → harder b/c no cues*

  use on written test

Prompt

Using points and details form the lecture, describe the two types of memory retrieval explained by the professor.

Response

The professor discusses two methods that people use when retrieving information from their mind. The first type of retrieval is called recognition. According to the professor, when you look at something familiar, your brain recognizes that it's something you've seen before. This type of memory retrieval is useful on multiple-choice tests. A more difficult type of memory retrieval is called recall. During recall, your brain must summon previously learned information without seeing it first. This is more difficult than recognition because your brain doesn't get any help when it recalls this information. You use this type of memory retrieval when taking a test that requires written answers.

TASK 1

Prompt

Who is your favorite character from a book or a movie? Describe this character and explain what you like about him or her. Use specific reasons and details to support your answer.

Preparation Time 00:00:15
Response Time 00:00:45

Notes

Opinion: ______________________________

- ______________________________
- ______________________________

Response

____

____

____

____

____

____

____

____

____

____

Prompt

A friend of yours has received some money; he plans to spend it on either a big vacation or a new car. Which of these two choices would you recommend for your friend? Use specific reasons in your answer.

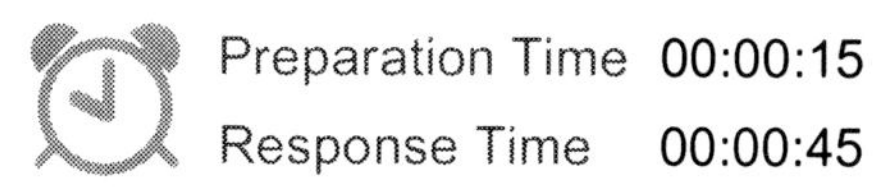

Notes

Preference: ______________________________

- ______________________________
- ______________________________

Response

____

____

____

____

____

____

____

____

____

____

Model Answer

Prompt

Who is your favorite character from a book or a movie? Describe this character and explain what you like about him or her. Use specific reasons and details to support your answer.

Notes

Opinion: *Samwise (*Lord of the Rings*)*

- *loyalty, sticks w/ Frodo*
- *bravery, never gives up*

Response

My favorite character, who appears in both films and novels, is Samwise Gamgee, a hobbit from the *Lord of the Rings* trilogy. In the story, he plays the best friend and travel companion of the protagonist, Frodo Baggins. One reason that I like Sam's character is that he remains loyal to his friend, Frodo, even as their journey across Middle Earth becomes increasingly difficult and dangerous. Even when Frodo tells him to leave, Sam continues to follow his friend. Additionally, Sam demonstrates his bravery on a number of occasions. Although he's small, Sam battles a giant spider and journeys into the enemy's kingdom to rescue Frodo. Ultimately, I like Sam's character because he embodies every quality that a good friend should have.

Model Answer

Prompt

A friend of yours has received some money; he plans to spend it on either a big vacation or a new car. Which of these two choices would you recommend for your friend? Use specific reasons in your answer.

Notes

Preference: *a big vacation*

- *cars require future maintenance/$*
- *maybe once-in-lifetime chance*

Response

If my friend were choosing between taking a big vacation and purchasing a new car, I would recommend that he take the vacation. One reason that he should take the vacation is that cars are a very long-term investment. Even after he buys the car, he'll still have to keep some of his money saved for future maintenance and for insurance. Additionally, having enough money to afford a big vacation might be a once-in-a-lifetime opportunity. He should take advantage of this chance to see someplace he has always dreamed of visiting, as he might not have so much money saved up again for a very long time.

UNIVERSITY ANNOUNCEMENT

New Campus Internet

State University is excited to announce that it will soon provide updated wireless Internet throughout campus. Currently, wireless Internet is only available in the library and the dorms. Moreover, because of an ever-increasing student population, the current wireless Internet is frequently slowed down by too many users, limiting Internet access for many students. The new Internet will not only be much faster, but it will also be available in the library, dorms, classrooms, and everywhere else on campus. However, State University must add 100 dollars per year to student tuition to make up for the increased cost of maintaining this new service.

Announcement Notes

Proposal: ______________________________

- ______________________________
- ______________________________

CONVERSATION

F: *I can't wait for the school to update their wireless Internet service.*

M: *It seems like a good idea, but I'm not sure paying 100 dollars a year is worth it.*

F: *I think it's a small price to pay. Think about it: right now you can only study in the dorms or at the library. But with the new Internet, you'll be able to study anywhere on campus. Imagine how pleasant it'll be to study outside on a sunny day!*

M: *Oh, yeah. I hadn't thought about the benefits of studying elsewhere on campus.*

F: *And anyway, the old wireless Internet was so slow and outdated. It'll be so nice to have fast, reliable Internet access. Maybe with this new Internet, I can even take study breaks to stream some good television shows or movies.*

M: *That's really true. The current Internet is too slow to do anything but research, and even that's difficult sometimes.*

F: *Exactly. Well, maybe now you have some reasons to get excited for that new wireless Internet after all.*

F: *Female Student* / **M:** *Male Student*

Conversation Notes

Speaker's opinion: ______________________________

- ______________________________
- ______________________________

Prompt

The female student expresses her opinion regarding the new wireless Internet. State her opinion and the reasons she gives for holding that opinion.

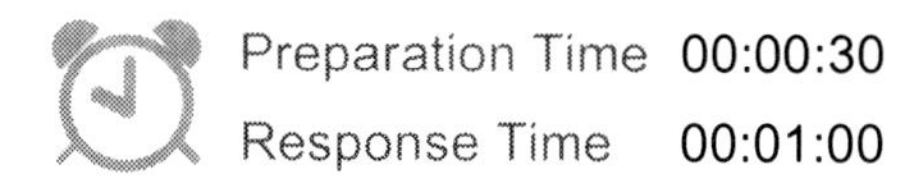

Use your 30 seconds of "Preparation Time" to organize your notes and prepare for your response.

Write your response on the lines below. Then **say your response aloud**, making sure that you can deliver your response within 1 minute.

Response

Model Answer

UNIVERSITY ANNOUNCEMENT

New Campus Internet

State University is excited to announce that it will soon provide updated wireless Internet throughout campus. Currently, wireless Internet is only available in the library and the dorms. Moreover, because of an ever-increasing student population, the current wireless Internet is frequently slowed down by too many users, limiting Internet access for many students. The new Internet will not only be much faster, but it will also be available in the library, dorms, classrooms, and everywhere else on campus. However, State University must add 100 dollars per year to student tuition to make up for the increased cost of maintaining this new service.

Announcement Notes

Proposal: *new campus-wide Wi-Fi*

- *too many students using current Wi-Fi*
- *pay $100/yr. for new Internet*

CONVERSATION

F: *I can't wait for the school to update their wireless Internet service.*

M: *It seems like a good idea, but I'm not sure paying 100 dollars a year is worth it.*

F: *I think it's a small price to pay. Think about it: right now you can only study in the dorms or at the library. But with the new Internet, you'll be able to study anywhere on campus. Imagine how pleasant it'll be to study outside on a sunny day!*

M: *Oh, yeah. I hadn't thought about the benefits of studying elsewhere on campus.*

F: *And anyway, the old wireless Internet was so slow and outdated. It'll be so nice to have fast, reliable Internet access. Maybe with this new Internet, I can even take study breaks to stream some good television shows or movies.*

M: *That's really true. The current Internet is too slow to do anything but research, and even that's difficult sometimes.*

F: *Exactly. Well, maybe now you have some reasons to get excited for that new wireless Internet after all.*

F: *Female Student* / ***M:*** *Male Student*

Conversation Notes

Speaker's opinion: *woman supports*

- *study anywhere, even outside*
- *↑ Wi-Fi speed, can stream TV, movies*

Prompt

The female student expresses her opinion regarding the new wireless Internet. State her opinion and the reasons she gives for holding that opinion.

Response

In the announcement, State University says that it'll update its on-campus wireless Internet. The new Internet will be available anywhere on campus, and it'll be much faster than the old Internet. However, it'll cost each student an additional 100 dollars a year to use. The woman in the conversation is in favor of the announcement for a couple of reasons. First, she's excited that the new Internet will allow her to work from anywhere on campus. She points out that the current Internet only works in the library and the dorms, but the new Internet will allow her to study outside if she wants. Second, she looks forward to having faster Internet access. She says that she might use the faster Internet to watch TV shows or movies when she's not studying.

PASSAGE

Islamic Art

Islamic art encompasses art created since the 7th century in areas inhabited or ruled by Islamic peoples. It includes secular and non-secular works, the majority of which is "decorative art" such as textiles, stonework, glass blowing, and illuminated manuscripts. Thus, Islamic art ranges from small, commonplace items to entire building exteriors. Most Islamic art of past centuries was created by middle-class artisans who often received funding from royal sponsors. Islamic artists borrowed techniques and inspirations from many sources, including Byzantine and early Christian artwork.

Passage Notes

Main Idea: ______________________________

▪ ______________________________

▪ ______________________________

LECTURE

Now that you have some background information, let's look at the cultural and religious significance of a couple of styles of Islamic art. Usually, Islamic religious art doesn't depict representations of humans or God because many Muslims believe that doing so is a form of idolatry, or worshiping representations of gods, which Islamic religious laws forbid. Thus, geographic patterns and calligraphy dominate Islamic art. Now I'll talk about some features of these two artistic styles.

Calligraphy, or decorative writing, is featured prominently in many religious paintings, but it's also found on secular, everyday objects such as coins, tile mosaics, and building exteriors. The majority of Islamic calligraphy is written in Arabic, but Persian and Turkish calligraphy appear in their respective regions. Calligraphy was so important to many Muslims because the Qur'an, the sacred religious text of Islam, was written in Arabic. So the Arabic language and writing are associated with God's words.

Additionally, Islamic artwork frequently uses geometric patterns, especially repeating sequences of squares and rectangles. For many Muslims, this use of repetitive, intricate patterns is meaningful; a pattern's repetition implies that it'll stretch on indefinitely, reflecting the infinite vastness of God's creation.

Lecture Notes

Topic: ______________________________

Example 1: ______________________________

▪ Details: ______________________________

Example 2: ______________________________

▪ Details: ______________________________

Prompt

Using details and examples from both the passage and the lecture, describe some of the key features of Islamic art, and explain their significance.

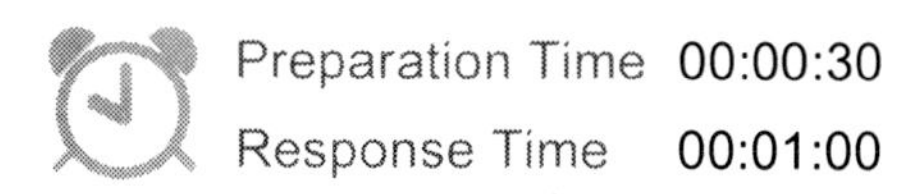

Use your 30 seconds of "Preparation Time" to organize your notes and prepare for your response.

Write your response on the lines below. Then **say your response aloud**, making sure that you can deliver your response within 1 minute.

Response

Model Answer

PASSAGE

Islamic Art

Islamic art encompasses art created since the 7th century in areas inhabited or ruled by Islamic peoples. It includes secular and non-secular works, the majority of which is "decorative art" such as textiles, stonework, glass blowing, and illuminated manuscripts. Thus, Islamic art ranges from small, commonplace items to entire building exteriors. Most Islamic art of past centuries was created by middle-class artisans who often received funding from royal sponsors. Islamic artists borrowed techniques and inspirations from many sources, including Byzantine and early Christian artwork.

Passage Notes

Main Idea: *Islamic art (7th c. +)*

- *both relig./non-relig., mostly decorative (textiles, glass)*
- *often made by mid-class artisans, influences = Byzantine, Christian*

LECTURE

Now that you have some background information, let's look at the cultural and religious significance of a couple of styles of Islamic art. Usually, Islamic religious art doesn't depict representations of humans or God because many Muslims believe that doing so is a form of idolatry, or worshiping representations of gods, which Islamic religious laws forbid. Thus, geographic patterns and calligraphy dominate Islamic art. Now I'll talk about some features of these two artistic styles.

Calligraphy, or decorative writing, is featured prominently in many religious paintings, but it's also found on secular, everyday objects such as coins, tile mosaics, and building exteriors. The majority of Islamic calligraphy is written in Arabic, but Persian and Turkish calligraphy appear in their respective regions. Calligraphy was so important to many Muslims because the Qur'an, the sacred religious text of Islam, was written in Arabic. So the Arabic language and writing are associated with God's words.

Additionally, Islamic artwork frequently uses geometric patterns, especially repeating sequences of squares and rectangles. For many Muslims, this use of repetitive, intricate patterns is meaningful; a pattern's repetition implies that it'll stretch on indefinitely, reflecting the infinite vastness of God's creation.

Lecture Notes

Topic: *styles of Islamic art*

Example 1: *calligraphy (fancy writing)*

- Details: *most Arabic (also Persian, Turk.), connects to Qur'an*

Example 2: *geometric patterns*

- Details: *lots of sq./rectangles, repetition = infinite, God*

Prompt

Using details and examples from both the passage and the lecture, describe some of the key features of Islamic art, and explain their significance.

Response

The reading passage discusses some major characteristics of Islamic art, which is art created in Islamic areas. Islamic art can be religious or non-religious, and most of it is decorative. Islamic art has been inspired by other cultures, such as the Byzantines, and other religions, such as Christianity. One common feature of Islamic art is calligraphy, which is intricate writing that's often in Arabic, the language of the Muslim holy book, the Qur'an. Many Muslims believe that this writing connects their art to God by relating to the Qur'an. Another common feature of Islamic art is the use of geometric patterns. For Muslims, the repetition of these patterns is supposed to represent the infinite, and the idea of the infinite links to God's creation of everything.

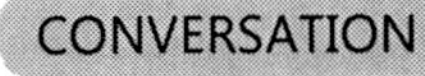

TASK 5

CONVERSATION

F: *How's it going, Jason?*

M: *Not too great, actually. The dining hall hours are driving me crazy this semester.*

F: *Why's that?*

M: *The dining hall closes at 9:00 pm every weekday, but I have classes from 6:00 pm until 9:30 pm on most days. I've had to go off campus and buy dinner almost every day this week. I can't afford to eat out every day, especially since I already have to pay for dining hall access.*

F: *Oh, man. I didn't realize you had class that late. Well, you could always buy a mini-refrigerator and a microwave. Then you can buy dinners from the grocery store that you can prepare in your dorm. Buying groceries is cheaper than dining out every night, at least.*

M: *I guess so, but I don't want to have to buy a fridge and a microwave. That still seems a bit pricey to me.*

F: *Well, have you heard about the dining hall's "Food To-go" program?*

M: *No, what's that?*

F: *If you go to the dining hall, you can pay a dollar for a small to-go box. You can fill that up with dinner before your classes and keep it in your dorm until you get back from class each night.*

M: *Oh wow, that could be useful and affordable. The food might be cold by the time I get to eat it, but it's definitely better than nothing.*

F: *Female Student* / **M:** *Male Student*

Conversation Notes

Speaker's problem: ______________________________

- Solution 1: ______________________________
- Solution 2: ______________________________

Prompt

Briefly summarize the problem the speakers are discussing. Then state which of the two solutions from the conversation you would recommend. Explain the reasons for your recommendation.

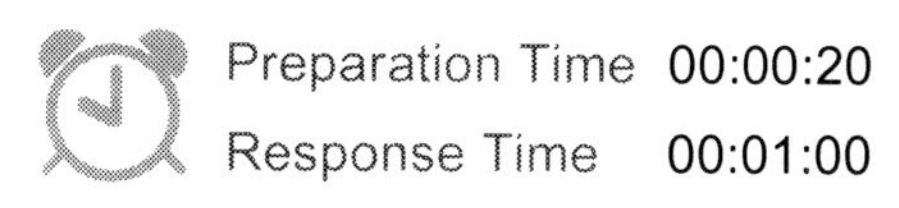

Use your 20 seconds of "Preparation Time" to organize your notes and prepare for your response.

Preparation Notes

Preferred solution: ______________________________

- Reason 1: ______________________________
- Reason 2: ______________________________

Write your response on the lines below. Then **say your response aloud**, making sure that you can deliver your response within 1 minute.

Response

Model Answer

CONVERSATION

F: *How's it going, Jason?*

M: *Not too great, actually. The dining hall hours are driving me crazy this semester.*

F: *Why's that?*

M: *The dining hall closes at 9:00 pm every weekday, but I have classes from 6:00 pm until 9:30 pm on most days. I've had to go off campus and buy dinner almost every day this week. I can't afford to eat out every day, especially since I already have to pay for dining hall access.*

F: *Oh, man. I didn't realize you had class that late. Well, you could always buy a mini-refrigerator and a microwave. Then you can buy dinners from the grocery store that you can prepare in your dorm. Buying groceries is cheaper than dining out every night, at least.*

M: *I guess so, but I don't want to have to buy a fridge and a microwave. That still seems a bit pricey to me.*

F: *Well, have you heard about the dining hall's "Food To-go" program?*

M: *No, what's that?*

F: *If you go to the dining hall, you can pay a dollar for a small to-go box. You can fill that up with dinner before your classes and keep it in your dorm until you get back from class each night.*

M: *Oh wow, that could be useful and affordable. The food might be cold by the time I get to eat it, but it's definitely better than nothing.*

F: Female Student / **M:** Male Student

Conversation Notes

Speaker's problem: *man → class conflicts w/ dining hall hrs.*

- Solution 1: *fridge + microwave + groceries for dorm*
- Solution 2: *dining hall "Food To-go" for $1*

Prompt

Briefly summarize the problem the speakers are discussing. Then state which of the two solutions from the conversation you would recommend. Explain the reasons for your recommendation.

Preparation Notes

Preferred solution: *sol. 2*

- Reason 1: *much more affordable*
- Reason 2: *save him a lot of time*

Response

The man's problem is that he has classes that prevent him from getting to the dining hall for dinner before it closes. The woman recommends that he either get some small appliances and food for his dorm, or that he use the dining hall's takeout program. Of the two proposed solutions, I think Jason should take advantage of the "Food To-go" program for a couple of reasons. For one, this option will be much more affordable than buying a refrigerator, a microwave, and food supplies for his dorm. Even if Jason uses the "Food To-go" program every day of the week, it'll only cost him 5 dollars extra per week. Additionally, the takeout program will save him a lot of time. Instead of having to leave campus and go to the store, he'll just have to walk over to the dining hall before his evening classes.

LECTURE

Film Music

Today we'll be exploring the question, "How does music contribute to a film?" But before we can answer this question, we must first determine what kind of film music we're talking about. So now let's discuss two types of film music: diegetic music and non-diegetic music.

Diegetic music originates from some source within the film's narrative. In other words, diegetic music is music that the film's characters can hear. For example, if a character in a film attends a concert, the sound of the band playing on stage is diegetic music. One purpose of diegetic music is to clarify the film's setting, such as where or when a film is taking place. Thus, if a character in a film plays hip-hop music on his car radio, the audience can generally assume that the film takes place in the present-day United States.

Non-diegetic music, then, doesn't come from any source within the film. Thus, characters in the film cannot hear non-diegetic music. Non-diegetic music much more common in films, and it's typically used to set the mood of a scene; it tells us how a character on screen feels, or how we should feel about a particular situation. For instance, an uplifting brass theme often plays when the hero of a story overcomes an obstacle or defeats an opponent.

Lecture Notes

Main Idea: ______________________________

Subtopic 1: ______________________________

- Details: ______________________________

____

Subtopic 2: ______________________________

- Details: ______________________________

____

Prompt

Using points and details form the lecture, describe the two types of film music explained by the professor.

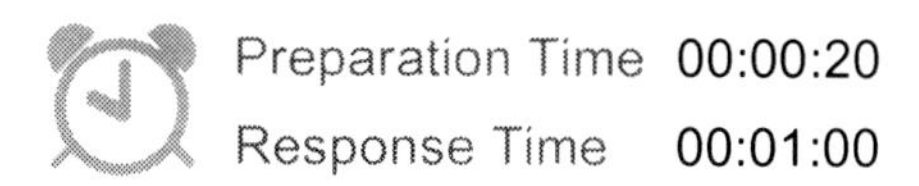

Use your 20 seconds of "Preparation Time" to organize your notes and prepare for your response.

Write your response on the lines below. Then **say your response aloud**, making sure that you can deliver your response within 1 minute.

Response

Model Answer

LECTURE

Film Music

Today we'll be exploring the question, "How does music contribute to a film?" But before we can answer this question, we must first determine what kind of film music we're talking about. So now let's discuss two types of film music: diegetic music and non-diegetic music.

Diegetic music originates from some source within the film's narrative. In other words, diegetic music is music that the film's characters can hear. For example, if a character in a film attends a concert, the sound of the band playing on stage is diegetic music. One purpose of diegetic music is to clarify the film's setting, such as where or when a film is taking place. Thus, if a character in a film plays hip-hop music on his car radio, the audience can generally assume that the film takes place in the present-day United States.

Non-diegetic music, then, doesn't come from any source within the film. Thus, characters in the film cannot hear non-diegetic music. Non-diegetic music much more common in films, and it's typically used to set the mood of a scene; it tells us how a character on screen feels, or how we should feel about a particular situation. For instance, an uplifting brass theme often plays when the hero of a story overcomes an obstacle or defeats an opponent.

Lecture Notes

Main Idea: *music in film*

Subtopic 1: *diegetic music*

- Details: *music in the film's "world";*
  chars. can hear, gives setting of film

Subtopic 2: *non-diegetic music*

- Details: *chars. can't hear (soundtrack);*
  sets mood, shows emotions

Prompt

Using points and details form the lecture, describe the two types of film music explained by the professor.

Response

The professor talks about two types of music that are often used in films: diegetic music and non-diegetic music. According to the lecture, diegetic music is music that is present in the film's story, so the characters of a film would be able to hear it. For example, if a character is singing in a movie, he or she is creating diegetic music. Diegetic music is sometimes meant to give information about where or when a film takes place. Non-diegetic music is what most people imagine when they think of a soundtrack, so it's music that the characters in a movie cannot hear. Usually, non-diegetic music is supposed to set the mood for a part of a movie or give information about the emotions that a character is feeling.

TASK 1

ACTUAL PRACTICE

Prompt

What one place would you recommend a tourist visit in your community, hometown, or city? Describe this place and explain why you would recommend visiting it. Use specific reasons and details to support your answer.

Preparation Time 00:00:15
Response Time 00:00:45

Notes

Opinion: ______________________

- ______________________
- ______________________

Response

____

____

____

____

____

____

____

____

____

____

Prompt

A university plans to develop a new research center in your community. Some people want a center for business research. Other people want a center for research in agriculture. Which of the two institutes would you recommend for your community? Use specific reasons in your answer.

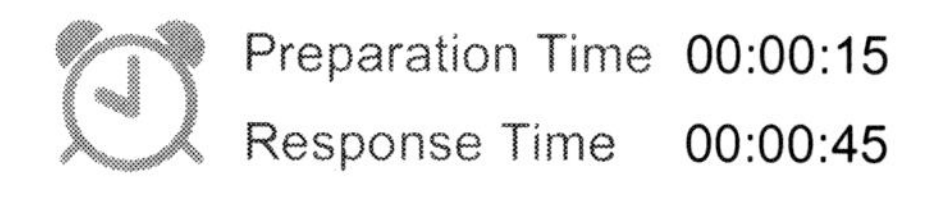

Notes

Preference: ____________________

- ____________________
- ____________________

Response

____

____

____

____

____

____

____

____

____

____

TASK 1

Model Answer

Prompt

What one place would you recommend a tourist visit in your community, hometown, or city? Describe this place and explain why you would recommend visiting it. Use specific reasons and details to support your answer.

Notes

Opinion: *visit Gyeongpo Beach*

- *friendly, relaxed atmosphere*
- *calm waters for floating, swimming*

Response

I would recommend that a tourist in my home city visit Gyeongpo Beach. For one, this beach is always filled with happy-looking families and friendly faces. For me, just being around so many people having fun makes me feel happier and more relaxed. Moreover, the clear waters at this beach are almost always calm, so this is a perfect spot to go for a nice, long swim or to just float in the water and absorb the warm sunlight. I have many happy memories from Gyeongpo Beach, and I'd gladly recommend it to anyone.

Model Answer

Prompt

A university plans to develop a new research center in your community. Some people want a center for business research. Other people want a center for research in agriculture. Which of the two institutes would you recommend for your community? Use specific reasons in your answer.

Notes

Preference: *agriculture-research school*

- *live in a rural area*
- *want to pursue agriculture*

Response

I would recommend that the university build an agriculture research facility in my hometown for a couple of reasons. First of all, this choice would be more appropriate for my community because I live in a very rural area. More than half the people in my community work in agriculture or livestock, so an agriculture research center would be a perfect fit. Additionally, I want to study agriculture in college, so a nearby agriculture research facility could be very useful for me. If I could study there, I'd be able to save a lot of money by living at home.

UNIVERSITY ANNOUNCEMENT

Recreational Classes to be Closed

As a result of budget cuts, State University will close its recreational physical education department next year. Consequently, the university will offer no official recreational classes for that period. Students will still have access to the gym, pool, tennis courts, baseball field, and other facilities on campus. However, they will have to organize activities at those facilities on their own time and without formal instruction. State University will save several million dollars by instituting this temporary program. The money saved will go toward necessary academic programs that have also been affected by budget cuts.

Announcement Notes

Proposal: ______________________________

- ______________________________
- ______________________________

CONVERSATION

F: *Hey, what do you think about the university not offering any recreational classes next year?*

M: *I'm not happy with that announcement. I really liked their martial arts classes. The instructors were great, and so was the exercise. I'm really going to miss not being able to take those classes next year.*

F: *Totally! I got almost all my exercise by taking the yoga and dance classes offered at the recreation center.*

M: *You know what else bothers me? The fact that the state government always makes us students suffer for its budgetary problems. I mean, it's not like we messed up the university's budget.*

F: *You're totally right. We pay to go here, so we should be able to decide which programs are affected by budget problems.*

M: *Definitely. And what about the fact that the university thinks of physical education as the least important department on campus?* (Sarcastic tone) *That just goes to show how much the university values our health.*

F: *Well, that's no surprise. You know the new university president is in love with math and engineering. So he probably thinks that every other department here is expendable.*

F: *Female Student* / **M:** *Male Student*

Conversation Notes

Speaker's opinion: ______________________________

- ______________________________
- ______________________________

Prompt

The male student expresses his opinion of the physical education department closure in the article. State his opinion and the reasons he gives for holding that opinion.

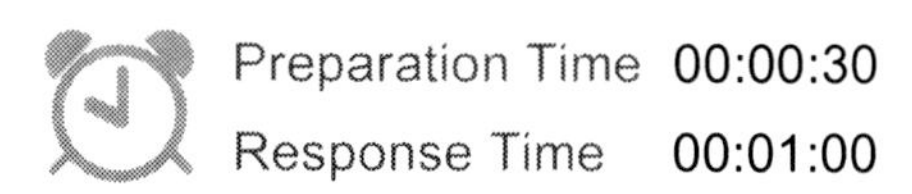

Use your 30 seconds of "Preparation Time" to organize your notes and prepare for your response.

Write your response on the lines below. Then **say your response aloud**, making sure that you can deliver your response within 1 minute.

Response

Model Answer

UNIVERSITY ANNOUNCEMENT

Recreational Classes to be Closed

As a result of budget cuts, State University will close its recreational physical education department next year. Consequently, the university will offer no official recreational classes for that period. Students will still have access to the gym, pool, tennis courts, baseball field, and other facilities on campus. However, they will have to organize activities at those facilities on their own time and without formal instruction. State University will save several million dollars by instituting this temporary program. The money saved will go toward necessary academic programs that have also been affected by budget cuts.

Announcement Notes

Proposal: *closing recreational PE department next yr.*

- *keep gym & ath. facilities open, but no classes*
- *save $ b/c of budget cuts*

CONVERSATION

F: *Hey, what do you think about the university not offering any recreational classes next year?*

M: *I'm not happy with that announcement. I really liked their martial arts classes. The instructors were great, and so was the exercise. I'm really going to miss not being able to take those classes next year.*

F: *Totally! I got almost all my exercise by taking the yoga and dance classes offered at the recreation center.*

M: *You know what else bothers me? The fact that the state government always makes us students suffer for its budgetary problems. I mean, it's not like we messed up the university's budget.*

F: *You're totally right. We pay to go here, so we should be able to decide which programs are affected by budget problems.*

M: *Definitely. And what about the fact that the university thinks of physical education as the least important department on campus?* (Sarcastic tone) *That just goes to show how much the university values our health.*

F: *Well, that's no surprise. You know the new university president is in love with math and engineering. So he probably thinks that every other department here is expendable.*

F: *Female Student* / **M:** *Male Student*

Conversation Notes

Speaker's opinion: *man opposes*

- *no martial arts, gov. shouldn't punish students for budget problems*
- *mad that univ. undervalues PE*

Prompt

The male student expresses his opinion of the physical education department closure in the article. State his opinion and the reasons he gives for holding that opinion.

Response

The university's announcement stated that the school will close its recreational PE department starting next academic year. The man opposes this announcement for a couple of reasons. First, the student says that he'll miss being able to take martial arts classes. He feels like the government always punishes the students when there are budget problems, even though the students aren't to blame. Second, he believes the university undervalues physical education because it's the first department to be closed because of budget cuts. He thinks the university needs to place more emphasis on students' health.

TASK 4

PASSAGE

Constructivism

In the field of education, the term "constructivism" refers to a theory of how people learn. As the name indicates, the theory of constructivism holds that individuals *construct* their own knowledge. Basically, people have a set of experiences and ideas about the world – an inner picture of how things work and what things mean. When they encounter something new, they try to make meaning of the information by fitting it into their inner picture. According to this theory, the best way to remember something is to have an active experience with it, such as talking about it with a friend, because experiences build knowledge.

Passage Notes

Main Idea: ______________________________

- ______________________________
- ______________________________

LECTURE

Okay, so before we look at how constructivism can be applied to education, let's look at a contrasting teaching method called "teacher-centered" education. Now, let's say you're a middle school math teacher, and your goal on a particular day is to teach a new mathematical formula to your students. One way you could do it would be to write the formula on the board, explain it, have the students copy it down, and then give them practice problems.

However, the theory of constructivism says that students are not really very likely to remember the formula if you present it that way. So a constructivist teacher would try a more "student-centered" approach. The teacher might introduce a word problem that could be solved using the formula, but not provide the formula. The teacher might then put the students into groups of three or four, and ask them to try to come up with a formula to solve the word problem. The teacher would have to walk around the class, paying attention to the groups' progress and giving a suggestion here or there to help them along. By the end of class, ideally all the students have figured it out with assistance from each other and the teacher. The formula will seem like a wonderful discovery and students will remember it well.

Lecture Notes

Topic: ______________________________

Example 1: ______________________________

- Details: ______________________________

Example 2: ______________________________

- Details: ______________________________

Prompt

Using details and examples from the lecture, explain how using constructivism theories in education differs from the "teacher-centered" method.

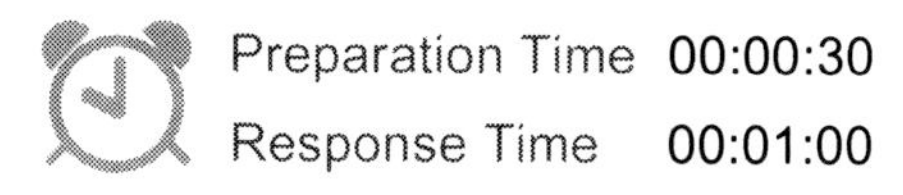

Use your 30 seconds of "Preparation Time" to organize your notes and prepare for your response.

Write your response on the lines below. Then **say your response aloud**, making sure that you can deliver your response within 1 minute.

Response

Model Answer

PASSAGE

Constructivism

In the field of education, the term "constructivism" refers to a theory of how people learn. As the name indicates, the theory of constructivism holds that individuals *construct* their own knowledge. Basically, people have a set of experiences and ideas about the world – an inner picture of how things work and what things mean. When they encounter something new, they try to make meaning of the information by fitting it into their inner picture. According to this theory, the best way to remember something is to have an active experience with it, such as talking about it with a friend, because experiences build knowledge.

Passage Notes

Main Idea: *constructivism = theory of how we learn*

- *construct own knowledge from exp.; try to fit new info. into "picture"*
- *best way to remember: active exp.*

LECTURE

Okay, so before we look at how constructivism can be applied to education, let's look at a contrasting teaching method called "teacher-centered" education. Now, let's say you're a middle school math teacher, and your goal on a particular day is to teach a new mathematical formula to your students. One way you could do it would be to write the formula on the board, explain it, have the students copy it down, and then give them practice problems.

However, the theory of constructivism says that students are not really very likely to remember the formula if you present it that way. So a constructivist teacher would try a more "student-centered" approach. The teacher might introduce a word problem that could be solved using the formula, but not provide the formula. The teacher might then put the students into groups of three or four, and ask them to try to come up with a formula to solve the word problem. The teacher would have to walk around the class, paying attention to the groups' progress and giving a suggestion here or there to help them along. By the end of class, ideally all the students have figured it out with assistance from each other and the teacher. The formula will seem like a wonderful discovery and students will remember it well.

Lecture Notes

Topic: *non-construct. vs. construct. teaching method*

Example 1: *"teacher-centered"*

- Details: *math formula → write on board, explain, stud. practice*

Example 2: *construct. teacher*

- Details: *word prob., no formula provided → students "discover" formula, remember it well*

Prompt

Using details and examples from the lecture, explain how using constructivism theories in education differs from the "teacher-centered" method.

Response

In the lecture, the professor illustrates the theory of constructivism with an example of how it can be applied in the classroom. But first, he describes the "teacher-centered" way of teaching a math formula to contrast two teaching methods. In the "teacher-centered" method, the teacher writes the formula on the board and the students copy it. Next, the teacher provides problems to practice using the formula. But using constructivism teaching methods, the teacher might provide students with a word problem and help them discover the formula by having them work in groups. By having the experience of trying to figure out the formula, the students will remember it better because the theory states that people construct knowledge based on experiences.

TASK 5

CONVERSATION

M: *Hey, Lauren, How's the beginning of your semester going?*

F: *Not so good, actually. I went to the school's bookstore to buy my textbooks for this semester, but I can't afford all of them. They're just too expensive.*

M: *I can relate to that! I had to spend hundreds on my engineering textbooks last semester. But you know, there are a couple of cheaper ways to get your textbooks.*

F: *Really?*

M: *Absolutely. For one, you can look online for used copies of all your books.*

F: *Hmm, I didn't really think about that. Are the used textbooks online much cheaper?*

M: *Yeah, they're usually about half the price of a new textbook. The only downside is the books are usually kind of damaged, and most of them are filled with past students' notes.*

F: *Well, that might be a bit annoying, but buying the books online seems like a good option.*

M: *The other way to access textbooks is through the library. They have almost every textbook, and you can use all of them for free.*

F: *That sounds great. Can I take the textbooks back to my dorm?*

M: *Well, no. All textbooks have to stay in the library, so you'll have to do all your studying there.*

F: *Well, it would still be nice to get free access to the textbooks. Thanks for your advice!*

M: *Male Student* / **F:** *Female Student*

Conversation Notes

Speaker's problem: ____________________

- Solution 1: ____________________
- Solution 2: ____________________

Prompt

Briefly summarize the problem the speakers are discussing. Then state which of the two solutions from the conversation you would recommend. Explain the reasons for your recommendation.

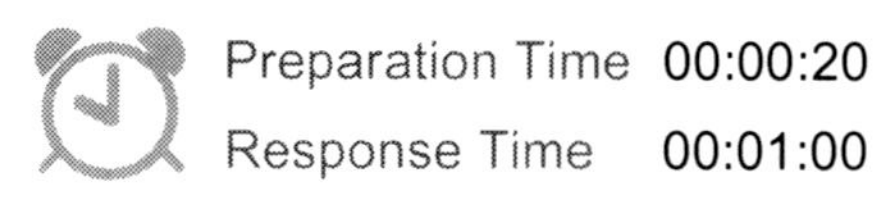

Use your 20 seconds of "Preparation Time" to organize your notes and prepare for your response.

Preparation Notes

Preferred solution: ______________________________

- Reason 1: ______________________________

- Reason 2: ______________________________

Write your response on the lines below. Then **say your response aloud,** making sure that you can deliver your response within 1 minute.

Response

____

____

____

____

____

____

____

____

____

____

TASK 5

ACTUAL PRACTICE 5

Model Answer

CONVERSATION

M: *Hey, Lauren, How's the beginning of your semester going?*

F: *Not so good, actually. I went to the school's bookstore to buy my textbooks for this semester, but I can't afford all of them. They're just too expensive.*

M: *I can relate to that! I had to spend hundreds on my engineering textbooks last semester. But you know, there are a couple of cheaper ways to get your textbooks.*

F: *Really?*

M: *Absolutely. For one, you can look online for used copies of all your books.*

F: *Hmm, I didn't really think about that. Are the used textbooks online much cheaper?*

M: *Yeah, they're usually about half the price of a new textbook. The only downside is the books are usually kind of damaged, and most of them are filled with past students' notes.*

F: *Well, that might be a bit annoying, but buying the books online seems like a good option.*

M: *The other way to access textbooks is through the library. They have almost every textbook, and you can use all of them for free.*

F: *That sounds great. Can I take the textbooks back to my dorm?*

M: *Well, no. All textbooks have to stay in the library, so you'll have to do all your studying there.*

F: *Well, it would still be nice to get free access to the textbooks. Thanks for your advice!*

M: *Male Student* / **F:** *Female Student*

Conversation Notes

Speaker's problem: *woman → textbooks too expensive*

- Solution 1: *shop for books online (abt. ½ price)*
- Solution 2: *use lib. copies of books (have to keep in lib.)*

Prompt

Briefly summarize the problem the speakers are discussing. Then state which of the two solutions from the conversation you would recommend. Explain the reasons for your recommendation.

Preparation Notes

Preferred solution: *sol. 2*

- Reason 1: *save her $*
- Reason 2: *clean, unmarked copies of textbooks*

Response

The woman's problem in the conversation is that she can't afford to purchase all her textbooks. The man recommends that she either shop for used copies of the books online or use the library's free copies. Personally, I think she should use the library's copies of the books. For one, using the libraries copies will save her a lot of money. Even if the woman found all her textbooks online, she'd still have to pay half the school's bookstore prices. Moreover, the library will have clean, unmarked copies of her textbooks. If she bought her books online, she might be distracted by old student notes or highlighting. And by using the library's copies, she'll have to study in the library, which is quiet and free of distractions.

LECTURE

Language Development

Scientists have long wondered how ancient humans developed language, the most complex form of communication in the animal kingdom. The way humans can turn random sounds into meaningful phrases and abstract concepts continues to puzzle researchers. However, understanding two areas of the brain, Wernicke's area and Broca's area, might provide some valuable clues.

Wernicke's area of the brain helps interpret the meaning of written and spoken language. In most people, Wernicke's area sits on the left side of the central part of the brain, near the auditory center. Those who suffer damage to this area of the brain suffer from a condition called Wernicke's aphasia; they can still form grammatically correct sentences, but they use irrelevant or nonexistent words, and they have trouble understanding other people's speech.

Broca's area is primarily used for speech production. The area was discovered by 19th-century physician Pierre Paul Broca. He noticed that two of his patients lost the ability to speak after injuring an area at the front-left part of the brain — he called this region Broca's area. Recently, researchers have linked Broca's area to the interpretation of gestures as well, possibly providing some insight into the origins of language. Some researchers suspect that Broca's area in early humans first developed to comprehend the symbolic meanings of gestures, but eventually, humans were able to assign meaning to abstract sounds (language) rather than gestures. Thus, processing spoken and written language may be an extension of our ability to interpret actions and gestures.

Lecture Notes

Main Idea: ____________________

Subtopic 1: ____________________

- Details: ____________________

____

Subtopic 2: ____________________

- Details: ____________________

____

Prompt

Using points and details form the lecture, explain the functions of Wernicke's area and Broca's area.

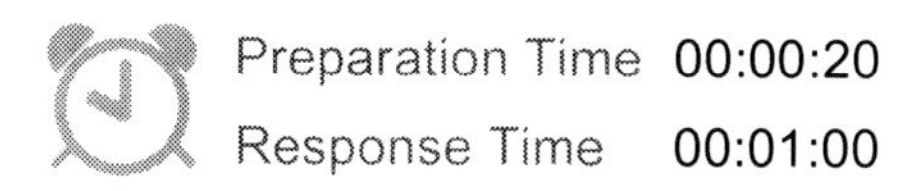

Use your 20 seconds of "Preparation Time" to organize your notes and prepare for your response.

Write your response on the lines below. Then **say your response aloud**, making sure that you can deliver your response within 1 minute.

Response

Model Answer

LECTURE

Language Development

Scientists have long wondered how ancient humans developed language, the most complex form of communication in the animal kingdom. The way humans can turn random sounds into meaningful phrases and abstract concepts continues to puzzle researchers. However, understanding two areas of the brain, Wernicke's area and Broca's area, might provide some valuable clues.

Wernicke's area of the brain helps interpret the meaning of written and spoken language. In most people, Wernicke's area sits on the left side of the central part of the brain, near the auditory center. Those who suffer damage to this area of the brain suffer from a condition called Wernicke's aphasia; they can still form grammatically correct sentences, but they use irrelevant or nonexistent words, and they have trouble understanding other people's speech.

Broca's area is primarily used for speech production. The area was discovered by 19th-century physician Pierre Paul Broca. He noticed that two of his patients lost the ability to speak after injuring an area at the front-left part of the brain — he called this region Broca's area. Recently, researchers have linked Broca's area to the interpretation of gestures as well, possibly providing some insight into the origins of language. Some researchers suspect that Broca's area in early humans first developed to comprehend the symbolic meanings of gestures, but eventually, humans were able to assign meaning to abstract sounds (language) rather than gestures. Thus, processing spoken and written language may be an extension of our ability to interpret actions and gestures.

Lecture Notes

Main Idea: *how humans form lang.*

Subtopic 1: *Wernicke's area*

- Details: *processes written/spoken lang., left-center brain;*

  damage = Wernicke's aphasia → can't use words correctly

Subtopic 2: *Broca's area*

- Details: *forming speech, front-left brain;*

  may interpret gestures (ancient use), developed later for lang.

Prompt

Using points and details form the lecture, explain the functions of Wernicke's area and Broca's area.

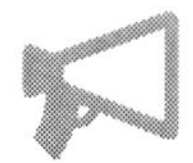

Response

The lecture discuses two parts of the human brain that are used to process and produce language. The first area of the brain discussed is Wernicke's area, which is located on left side of the center of the brain. This area processes written and spoken language, so when it becomes injured, a person will lose the ability to use words correctly, even though they can still form sentences. The other area of the brain discussed in the lecture is called Broca's area, and it is located on the left side of the front of the brain in most people. The Broca's area is used mostly to form speech. However, researchers have discovered that it may also interpret gestures, which may have been useful among humans before they used spoken language.

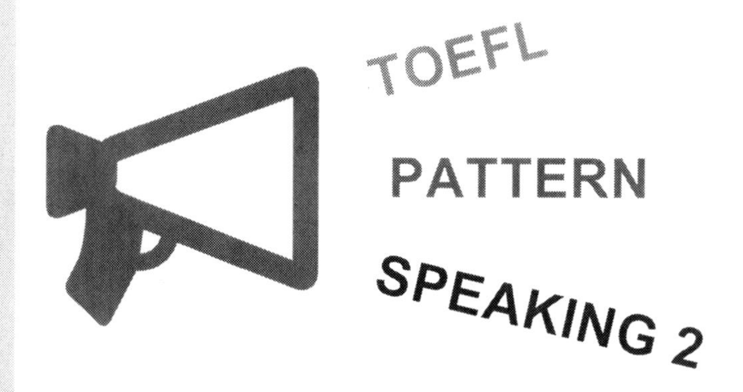

CHAPTER 8

Actual Test

1

Prompt

Discuss a time when you were injured or sick. What happened, and what help did you receive? Use specific reasons and examples to support your answer.

Preparation Time 00:00:15
Response Time 00:00:45

Notes

Response

Prompt

Some people feel that human activities are harming Earth. Others feel that human activities make Earth a better place to live. What is your opinion? Use specific reasons and examples to support your answer.

Preparation Time	00:00:15
Response Time	00:00:45

Notes

Response

TASK 3

UNIVERSITY ANNOUNCEMENT

Improved Tutoring Services

Next year, the university is going to expand its tutoring services. In addition to offering tutoring in core subjects such as writing, math, foreign languages, and the sciences, the university will also offer tutoring for computer science, engineering, the social sciences, and business. The university administration wants to offer more tutoring services in order to improve students' academic performances and help students fully understand their course material. In recent years, the average student's grade point average (GPA) has dropped while the number of complaints related to class difficulty has increased. Hopefully, these issues will be remedied by expanding the range of our tutoring services.

CONVERSATION

F: *I don't think the university's going to solve many problems by expanding the tutoring center.*

M: *Why do you say that? Offering more tutoring seems like the best way to solve any student-GPA issues.*

F: *Well, for one, most students don't struggle in the classes that the university is going to add to the tutoring schedule.*

M: *Really? What subjects do students struggle in, then?*

F: *Most students have trouble in their general education classes. You know, like math and writing.*

M: *But doesn't the school already offer tutoring help for those subjects?*

F: *Exactly! So why should we bother adding tutoring help for classes very few students need help in.*

M: *I see your point. But why have student GPAs gone down in recent years? Surely more tutoring will help improve student GPAs a little.*

F: *Actually, I don't think it will. The decrease in GPAs has more to do with the fact that it has become easier to get into State University over the past couple years. Instead of expanding the tutoring center, the university really needs to make admissions requirements stricter. Then maybe we'll see an improvement in GPAs.*

F: *Female Student* / **M:** *Male Student*

Notes

Prompt

The woman expresses her opinion about the plan described in the announcement. Briefly summarize the plan. Then state her opinion about the plan and explain her reasons for holding that opinion.

Preparation Time	00:00:30
Response Time	00:01:00

Response

TASK

4

PASSAGE

Planets

A celestial body must fulfill three qualifications before it can be considered a planet. For one, the celestial body must orbit a star or the remains of an expired star. Furthermore, the object must be massive enough to become rounded by its own gravity. In other words, a planet must be heavy enough to create a gravitational pull that draws all material on that planet toward the planet's center; if all material gets as close to the center as possible, the end result is a sphere. Finally, a planet must clear its orbit of all debris, ensuring that it is the largest object in the surrounding area.

LECTURE

Now that you've read about some basic qualities of planets, I'd like to draw a distinction between the types of planets that astronomers have observed. So now let's look at some differences between terrestrial planets and gas giants.

In our solar system, there are four terrestrial planets: Mercury, Venus, Earth, and Mars. In addition to being the four planets closest to the Sun, these planets are all composed of rocky or metallic elements. Thus, terrestrial planets have solid surfaces as well as geographical features such as canyons and volcanoes. Additionally, terrestrial planets are smaller than gas giants, so they usually have a weaker gravitational pull and thus fewer moons.

Gas giants don't contain any metallic or rocky elements. They're composed entirely of gases. Most observable gas giants located in other solar systems are composed of hydrogen and helium, much like Jupiter or Saturn. But some gaseous planets, such as Neptune and Uranus, are made of heavier elements such as methane and ammonia. Although their gaseous composition makes them less dense than terrestrial planets, the smallest gas giant in our solar system, Uranus, is larger than the largest terrestrial planet, Earth. Thus, gas giants have a strong gravitational field, meaning that many moons as well as rings of smaller celestial objects usually orbit gas giants.

Notes

Prompt

Using the information from the reading and the lecture, describe some of the similarities an differences between terrestrial planets and gas giants.

Preparation Time 00:00:30
Response Time 00:01:00

Response

TASK

5

CONVERSATION

A: *How can I help you today?*

FS: *I had a late registration time this semester, and by the time I was able to register for classes, all the ones I need for my major were already full.*

A: *Ah, I see. Many students have this problem, but there are some options. Like, have you finished your general education requirements yet? If not, you can always sign up for those classes; GE classes usually have openings.*

FS: *Yeah, I guess I could do that, but then I'll be a semester behind everyone else in my major because they'll be in upper-division classes while I'm just getting started with my lower-division classes.*

A: *Well, in that case, you can also try to "crash" the classes you feel you absolutely need to take this semester.*

FS: *"Crash" a class. What do you mean?*

A: *Just go to the classes you want to get into on the first day of class. After class is over, ask the professor if any students have already dropped the class or didn't show up for the first lecture. If there are some absent or dropped students, the professor will probably let you take their place.*

FS: *I hope there are some openings in at least a couple of the classes I need to take. Thanks for your help.*

A: *No problem. As an academic advisor, that's what I'm here for.*

A: Advisor / **FS:** Female Student

Notes

Prompt

Briefly summarize the problem the speakers are discussing. Then state which of the two solutions from the conversation you would recommend. Explain the reasons for your recommendation.

Preparation Time 00:00:20
Response Time 00:01:00

Response

6

LECTURE

Island Biology

Islands contain some of the most biologically diverse habitats on Earth. Because islands are often inaccessible to many larger creatures that can't fly or float to them, islands may have more ecological niches that need to be filled, so island species evolve special adaptations to fill these niches. Many island species adapt to fill a different ecological role than their mainland ancestors, often through either island gigantism or insular dwarfism.

Island gigantism occurs when some island species evolve to be much larger than their mainland equivalents. This often occurs because islands are inaccessible to large, mammalian predators. Thus, small reptilian and avian predatory species will evolve to become much larger so they can fill the niche left empty by a lack of large predators. But because these large avian and reptilian predators aren't as efficient at predation as the mammalian predators they replaced, many prey species can grow larger because of decreased predation. Therefore, island gigantism explains why the large, flightless, and defenseless dodo bird thrived on the island of Mauritius in the Indian Ocean until its sudden extinction caused by overhunting.

As its name implies, insular dwarfism describes the process by which some large species become smaller when they evolve on an island. One of the largest factors that contribute to insular dwarfism is limited resources for both carnivore and herbivore species. When a large island-dwelling species begins to deplete the island's natural resources, the smallest members of the species are likely to survive because they require the least amount of food and territory. The small survivors will pass their genes for smallness to their offspring, leading to an overall decrease in the size of the species. For example, on the Indonesian island of Flores, researchers have discovered archaeological evidence of an extinct cousin species to humans that stood less than 4 feet tall. Researchers suspect that this species, called Homo *floresiensis, was isolated on Flores for thousands of years, causing the species to undergo insular dwarfism and become smaller than other hominids.*

Notes

Prompt

Using points and examples from the talk, explain some of the unique features that may develop among island-dwelling animal species.

Preparation Time 00:00:20
Response Time 00:01:00

Response

Model Answer

Prompt

Discuss a time when you were injured or sick. What happened, and what help did you receive? Use specific reasons and examples to support your answer.

Notes

opinion: playing soccer → twist ankle

1) coach carried me off field

2) parents brought me ice

Response

A time I remember when I was injured was while playing soccer in middle school. I was playing forward on my school's team. We were hosting a game at our school, but unfortunately our field was covered with small gopher holes. So, in the second half I was running to receive an assist when my foot went into a hole and I fell, painfully twisting my ankle. My coach helped me by carrying me "piggyback" off the field, even though I was bigger than she was. I went home and lay down on the couch, where my parents brought me ice and food for a few boring days until I was up again and, of course, playing soccer.

Model Answer

Prompt

Some people feel that human activities are harming Earth. Others feel that human activities make Earth a better place to live. What is your opinion? Use specific reasons and examples to support your answer.

Notes

humans harming Earth

1) greenhouse gas from cars → life more diff.

2) pollution/overfishing harms ocean

Response

I believe that many human activities are harming the Earth and its inhabitants. Humans undertake many activities that produce huge amounts of greenhouse gases. For example, almost all cars release carbon dioxide, which stores up in the atmosphere and traps heat. The heating of Earth's surface will cause the polar ice caps to melt, which will make Earth a more difficult place to live due to rising sea levels and harsher weather. Also, humans constantly pollute the oceans by dumping garbage and allowing oil spills to occur. These factors, in addition to overfishing, threaten the existence of countless ocean species, and oceans cover two-thirds of the planet. Thus, human activities threaten the future of our planet.

TASK

3

Model Answer

UNIVERSITY ANNOUNCEMENT

Improved Tutoring Services

Next year, the university is going to expand its tutoring services. In addition to offering tutoring in core subjects such as writing, math, foreign languages, and the sciences, the university will also offer tutoring for computer science, engineering, the social sciences, and business. The university administration wants to offer more tutoring services in order to improve students' academic performances and help students fully understand their course material. In recent years, the average student's grade point average (GPA) has dropped while the number of complaints related to class difficulty has increased. Hopefully, these issues will be remedied by expanding the range of our tutoring services.

CONVERSATION

F: *I don't think the university's going to solve many problems by expanding the tutoring center.*

M: *Why do you say that? Offering more tutoring seems like the best way to solve any student-GPA issues.*

F: *Well, for one, most students don't struggle in the classes that the university is going to add to the tutoring schedule.*

M: *Really? What subjects do students struggle in, then?*

F: *Most students have trouble in their general education classes. You know, like math and writing.*

M: *But doesn't the school already offer tutoring help for those subjects?*

F: *Exactly! So why should we bother adding tutoring help for classes very few students need help in.*

M: *I see your point. But why have student GPAs gone down in recent years? Surely more tutoring will help improve student GPAs a little.*

F: *Actually, I don't think it will. The decrease in GPAs has more to do with the fact that it has become easier to get into State University over the past couple years. Instead of expanding the tutoring center, the university really needs to make admissions requirements stricter. Then maybe we'll see an improvement in GPAs.*

F: *Female Student* / **M:** *Male Student*

Notes

proposal: tutoring in + subjects

- *↑ GPAs and class comprehension*

speaker's opinion: woman opposes

- *most students bad in GE classes (already tutoring for those)*
- *real problem → too easy to get into univ. (make admission harder for ↑ GPAs)*

Model Answer

Prompt

The woman expresses her opinion about the plan described in the announcement. Briefly summarize the plan. Then state her opinion about the plan and explain her reasons for holding that opinion.

Response

The university's announcement states that it'll start offering tutoring in a wider variety of subjects. Thus, it'll offer tutoring in major-specific fields, such as engineering and business. The woman says that this will probably not bring up students grades. One reason she believes this is because most students seem to struggle in their general education classes, which the school already has tutoring for. Therefore, she believes that the expanded tutoring is a waste of money. Moreover, she claims that the real cause of students' decreasing GPAs is that the admission requirements have become too easy. According to her, if the university becomes more selective, then overall student GPAs will improve.

TASK

4

Model Answer

PASSAGE

Planets

A celestial body must fulfill three qualifications before it can be considered a planet. For one, the celestial body must orbit a star or the remains of an expired star. Furthermore, the object must be massive enough to become rounded by its own gravity. In other words, a planet must be heavy enough to create a gravitational pull that draws all material on that planet toward the planet's center; if all material gets as close to the center as possible, the end result is a sphere. Finally, a planet must clear its orbit of all debris, ensuring that it is the largest object in the surrounding area.

LECTURE

Now that you've read about some basic qualities of planets, I'd like to draw a distinction between the types of planets that astronomers have observed. So now let's look at some differences between terrestrial planets and gas giants.

In our solar system, there are four terrestrial planets: Mercury, Venus, Earth, and Mars. In addition to being the four planets closest to the Sun, these planets are all composed of rocky or metallic elements. Thus, terrestrial planets have solid surfaces as well as geographical features such as canyons and volcanoes. Additionally, terrestrial planets are smaller than gas giants, so they usually have a weaker gravitational pull and thus fewer moons.

Gas giants don't contain any metallic or rocky elements. They're composed entirely of gases. Most observable gas giants located in other solar systems are composed of hydrogen and helium, much like Jupiter or Saturn. But some gaseous planets, such as Neptune and Uranus, are made of heavier elements such as methane and ammonia. Although their gaseous composition makes them less dense than terrestrial planets, the smallest gas giant in our solar system, Uranus, is larger than the largest terrestrial planet, Earth. Thus, gas giants have a strong gravitational field, meaning that many moons as well as rings of smaller celestial objects usually orbit gas giants.

Notes

P: planet requirements

- *(1) orbit star, (2) gravity makes it round, (3) must have clear orbit*

L: terrestrial vs. gaseous planets

- *terrestrial → Mercury, Venus, Earth, Mars; rocky/metal, solid surface, geo. features*
- *gaseous → Jupiter, Saturn, Uranus, Neptune; all gas, ↓ dense, ↑ mass, ↑ moons*

Prompt

Using the information from the reading and the lecture, describe some of the similarities an differences between terrestrial planets and gas giants.

Response

The passage gives some basic information about what qualities every planet has. It has to orbit a star, be heavy enough to become rounded by gravity, and have a clear and uninterrupted orbit. The lecture then divides planets into two categories: terrestrial planets and gas giants. Terrestrial planets, such as Earth or Mars, are made of rocky or metallic elements. Thus, they have solid surfaces and geological features like valleys and mountains. Gas giants like Jupiter and Saturn, on the other hand, are made of gaseous elements such as hydrogen and helium. Gas giants are less dense but more massive than terrestrial planets, and gas giants usually have more moons. In our solar system, the terrestrial planets formed closer to the Sun, while the gas giants formed further away.

Model Answer

CONVERSATION

A: *How can I help you today?*

FS: *I had a late registration time this semester, and by the time I was able to register for classes, all the ones I need for my major were already full.*

A: *Ah, I see. Many students have this problem, but there are some options. Like, have you finished your general education requirements yet? If not, you can always sign up for those classes; GE classes usually have openings.*

FS: *Yeah, I guess I could do that, but then I'll be a semester behind everyone else in my major because they'll be in upper-division classes while I'm just getting started with my lower-division classes.*

A: *Well, in that case, you can also try to "crash" the classes you feel you absolutely need to take this semester.*

FS: *"Crash" a class. What do you mean?*

A: *Just go to the classes you want to get into on the first day of class. After class is over, ask the professor if any students have already dropped the class or didn't show up for the first lecture. If there are some absent or dropped students, the professor will probably let you take their place.*

FS: *I hope there are some openings in at least a couple of the classes I need to take. Thanks for your help.*

A: *No problem. As an academic advisor, that's what I'm here for.*

A: Advisor / **FS:** Female Student

Notes

problem → classes for major full

sol. 1 → finish GE classes instead

sol. 2 → crash class, take other student's spot

preferred sol. → sol. 1

reason 1 → impt. to complete GEs early

reason 2 → if crash fails, behind in all classes

Prompt

Briefly summarize the problem the speakers are discussing. Then state which of the two solutions from the conversation you would recommend. Explain the reasons for your recommendation.

Response

The problem being discussed by the student and advisor is that the student was unable to get into any of the classes that she needs to complete her major. The advisor recommends that she either take general education classes instead, or that she try to "crash" the classes and get an absent student's spot. I think she should just sign up for general education classes for a couple of reasons. First of all, I've been told that it's better to get your general education classes finished as soon as possible. That way you don't have to worry about taking them once you get really involved in your major. Additionally, if she did decide to "crash" the classes but didn't get into them, she'd still have to sign up for general education classes, but she'll have missed the first few classes. Her grades might suffer as a result.

TASK

6

Model Answer

LECTURE

Island Biology

Islands contain some of the most biologically diverse habitats on Earth. Because islands are often inaccessible to many larger creatures that can't fly or float to them, islands may have more ecological niches that need to be filled, so island species evolve special adaptations to fill these niches. Many island species adapt to fill a different ecological role than their mainland ancestors, often through either island gigantism or insular dwarfism.

Island gigantism occurs when some island species evolve to be much larger than their mainland equivalents. This often occurs because islands are inaccessible to large, mammalian predators. Thus, small reptilian and avian predatory species will evolve to become much larger so they can fill the niche left empty by a lack of large predators. But because these large avian and reptilian predators aren't as efficient at predation as the mammalian predators they replaced, many prey species can grow larger because of decreased predation. Therefore, island gigantism explains why the large, flightless, and defenseless dodo bird thrived on the island of Mauritius in the Indian Ocean until its sudden extinction caused by overhunting.

As its name implies, insular dwarfism describes the process by which some large species become smaller when they evolve on an island. One of the largest factors that contribute to insular dwarfism is limited resources for both carnivore and herbivore species. When a large island-dwelling species begins to deplete the island's natural resources, the smallest members of the species are likely to survive because they require the least amount of food and territory. The small survivors will pass their genes for smallness to their offspring, leading to an overall decrease in the size of the species. For example, on the Indonesian island of Flores, researchers have discovered archaeological evidence of an extinct cousin species to humans that stood less than 4 feet tall. Researchers suspect that this species, called Homo floresiensis, was isolated on Flores for thousands of years, causing the species to undergo insular dwarfism and become smaller than other hominids.

Notes

main idea: island ecology → very diverse, many niches to fill

subtopic 1: island gigantism

island species grow ↑, no predator mammals = big predator birds/reptiles;

predators not as efficient → prey gets bigger (dodo)

subtopic 2: insular dwarfism

island species grow ↓ b/c of limited resources;

*smallest members of species survive (*Homo floresiensis*)*

Prompt

Using points and examples from the talk, explain some of the unique features that may develop among island-dwelling animal species.

Response

The professor talks about some of the ways that animals adapt to an island habitat. First, he describes a process called island gigantism, which occurs when a species on an island grows larger than similar species on a mainland. Usually, this occurs because predatory mammals aren't on the island, so reptiles and birds fill this predator niche. But because these new predators aren't as effective as mammals, the prey species can also grow large on the island. The dodo bird is an example of a prey species that grew large because of a lack of predators. Next, the professor talks about insular dwarfism, which occurs when limited food resources on an island cause only the smallest members of a species to survive. The professor talks about an extinct species related to humans that were isolated on an island in Indonesia. This isolation caused them to become smaller than other species of humans.

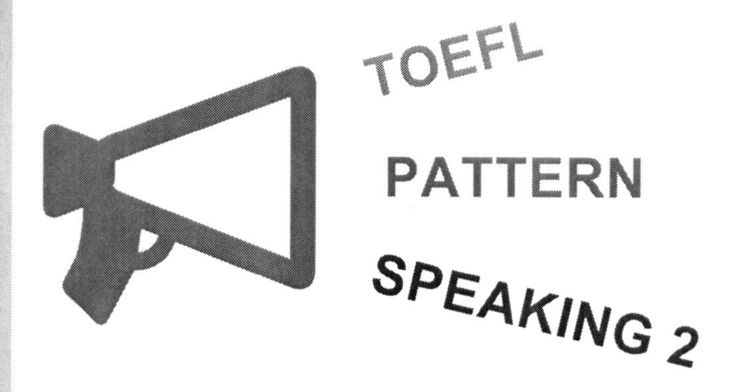

APPENDIX

Answer Key

▶ Note: All listed answers are examples; responses will vary.

CHAPTER 1

p. 7

PRACTICE 1 (*Answers will vary.*)

2) My favorite movie is ***The Lion King*** because **I find the story uplifting and inspiring.**
3) My favorite color is **red** because **it reminds me of romance.**
4) My favorite author is **Oscar Wilde** because **he makes witty observations about society.**
5) My favorite subject in school is **history** because **it helps me understand how cultures change.**
6) My favorite animal is **the elephant** because **it is a huge yet gentle and intelligent creature.**
7) My favorite season is **summer** because **I get to go on a family vacation.**
8) My favorite city is **Kyoto** because **it has serene and relaxing gardens.**

PRACTICE 2 (*Answers will vary.*)

1) go to father for advice
2) going to fair w/ fam.
3) Michael Jordan

p. 9

PRACTICE 1 (*Answers will vary.*)

1) **Opinion**: go to father for advice
   TS: When I'm faced with a difficult problem, I usually ask my father for advice.
2) **Opinion**: going to fair w/ fam.
   TS: One of my earliest childhood memories is going to the fair with my family when I was seven years old.
3) **Opinion**: Michael Jordan
   TS: One famous person who I've always admired is retired athlete Michael Jordan.

p. 11

PRACTICE 1 (*Answers will vary.*)

1) **TS**: When I'm faced with a difficult problem, I usually ask my father for advice.
   ▸ **NOTES**
   Reason 1: faced the same problems as me
   Reason 2: doesn't judge; understanding
2) **TS**: One of my earliest childhood memories is going to the fair with my family when I was seven years old.
   ▸ **NOTES**
   Reason 1: saw animals/had never seen before
   Reason 2: time when whole fam. was together
3) **TS**: One famous person who I've always admired is retired athlete Michael Jordan.
   ▸ **NOTES**
   Reason 1: ath. talented (basketball, baseball, golf)
   Reason 2: kind, met him in person

p. 13

PRACTICE 1 (*Answers will vary.*)

1) **Opinion**: go to father for advice
   TS: When I am faced with a difficult problem, I usually ask my father for advice.
   Reason 1: faced the same problems as me
   Reason 2: doesn't judge, understanding
   Rs: When I'm faced with a difficult problem, I usually ask my father for advice for a couple of reasons. First, I know that my dad has faced many of the same challenges as me when he was growing up. His advice is always really helpful because it comes from his own experiences. Also, my father is a very patient, understanding person, so I can always count on him to listen to my problems. He never judges me or dismisses my problems as trivial or unimportant. For these reasons, I value my father's advice more than anyone else's.

p. 14

PRACTICE 2 (*Answers will vary.*)

1) **Opinion**: going to fair w/ fam.
   TS: One of my earliest childhood memories is going to the fair with my family when I was seven years old.
   Reason 1: saw animals/had never seen before
   Reason 2: time when whole fam. was together
   Rs: One of my earliest childhood memories is going to the fair with my family when I was seven years old. There are two reasons that this memory is so special to me. For one, I had never seen many of the animals that were at the fair before. Because I was just seven years old when we went, I thought that the cows at the fair must have been the biggest animals in the world. Another reason the memory is so special to me is because it was one of the few times my whole family was together. My father traveled for business a lot, and my older brother was often away at boarding school, so visiting the fair with everyone together made for a special day.

p. 15

PRACTICE 3 (*Answers will vary.*)

1) **Opinion**: Michael Jordan
   TS: One famous person who I've always admired is retired athlete Michael Jordan.

Reason 1: athletically talented (basketball, baseball, golf)

Reason 2: kind, met him in person

Rs: One famous person who I've always admired is retired athlete Michael Jordan. One reason I admire Michael Jordan is that he is an incredibly talented athlete. He is arguably the greatest basketball player to ever live, and he also played professional baseball and golf. Moreover, he is a very kind person who is respectful to his fans. When I visited Chicago when I was young, I had the opportunity to meet Michael Jordan very briefly. He was very polite to me and my family, and he signed my basketball jersey.

CHAPTER 2

p. 31

PRACTICE 1 (*Possible answers for both sides are given.*)

2) **Side 1**: I would prefer to live in **an urban area** because **I like to be around lots of people**.

   Side 2: I would prefer to live in **a rural area** because **I enjoy being outdoors in nature**.

3) **Side 1**: I would rather **read a book** because **reading encourages me to use my imagination**.

   Side 2: I would rather **watch a movie** because **reading is too time-consuming**.

4) **Side 1**: I prefer to **stay up late** because **I like to go out and socialize with my friends at night**.

   Side 2: I prefer to **wake up early** because **I am more productive in the morning**.

PRACTICE 2 (*Answers will vary.*)

1) get enough sleep
2) fuel efficiency
3) no electronics in class

p. 33

PRACTICE 1 (*Answers will vary.*)

1) **Preference**: get enough sleep

   TS: When preparing for a test, I never stay up all night studying because I prefer to be well rested.

2) **Preference**: fuel efficiency

   TS: When looking for a new car, I value fuel efficiency over a powerful engine.

3) **Preference**: no electronics in class

   TS: Although some people prefer using electronics in class, I prefer taking classes where the instructor does not allow students to use electronics.

p. 35

PRACTICE 1 (*Answers will vary.*)

1) **TS**: When preparing for a test, I never stay up all night studying because I prefer to be well rested.

   ▸ **NOTES**

   Reason 1: well rested → more prepared

   Reason 2: don't remember last min. info.

2) **TS**: When looking for a new car, I value fuel efficiency over a powerful engine.

   ▸ **NOTES**

   Reason 1: speed limit → no need big engine

   Reason 2: enjoy saving $

3) **TS**: Although some people prefer using electronics in class, I prefer taking classes where the instructor does not allow students to use electronics.

   ▸ **NOTES**

   Reason 1: less distraction

   Reason 2: notes by hand → remember better

p. 37

PRACTICE 1 (*Answers will vary.*)

1) **Preference**: receiving help from profs.

   TS: When preparing for a test, I never stay up all night studying because I prefer to be well rested for the test.

   Reason 1: well rested → more prepared

   Reason 2: don't remember last min. info.

   Rs: When preparing for a test, I never stay up all night studying because I prefer to be well rested. I'd rather miss a few hours of studying and feel well rested and energized for a test than feel exhausted because I stayed up all night studying. Moreover, I don't usually remember most of the information when I try to stay up all night preparing. I once failed a math test because I stayed up all night memorizing formulas. When I took the test the next day, I was too tired to recall most of the formulas I had worked so hard to memorize just hours earlier.

p. 38

PRACTICE 2 (*Answers will vary.*)

1) **Preference**: fuel efficiency

   TS: When looking for a new car, I value fuel efficiency over a powerful engine.

   Reason 1: speed limit → no need big engine

   Reason 2: enjoy saving $

   Rs: When looking for a new car, I value fuel efficiency over a powerful engine. Because I'm always afraid of being pulled over for speeding, I see no point in buying an expensive, fast car. I would never bother trying to take the car to its top speed for fear of getting a speeding ticket, so I'd rather have a car with a smaller engine that gets good gas mileage. Additionally, I'm very careful with my spending habits, so I hate having to fill my car up with expensive gasoline. For these reasons, I'd much rather buy a fuel-efficient car than a high-performance sports car.

p. 39

PRACTICE 3 (*Answers will vary.*)

1) **Preference**: no electronics in class

TS: Although some people prefer using electronics in class, I prefer taking classes where the instructor does not allow students to use electronics.

Reason 1: less distraction

Reason 2: notes by hand → remember better

Rs: Although some people prefer using electronics in class, I prefer taking classes where the instructor does not allow electronics. I have this preference for a couple of reasons. First, I'm less distracted when I cannot bring my computer to class. If I try to use my computer for note-taking, I'm always tempted to browse the Internet instead of focusing on my instructor. Second, I'd rather write my notes by hand than type them on a computer. I believe that writing notes by hand helps with memorization because it uses kinetic memory.

CHAPTER 3

p. 55

PRACTICE 1 (*Answers will vary.*)

Proposal: close game room, expand bowl. alley

Reason 1: games outdated, not buying new

Reason 2: few students use

p. 57

PRACTICE 1 (*Answers will vary.*)

Opinion: woman supports

Reason 1: game rooms → "old fashioned"

Reason 2: play games on web instead

p. 59

PRACTICE 1 (*Answers will vary.*)

1) **From Notes → Proposal**: close game room → outdated, few use

2) **From Notes → Opinion**: woman supports

3) **From Notes → Reason 1**: game rooms → "old-fashioned"

Reason 2: play games on web instead

p. 61

PRACTICE 1 (*Answers will vary.*)

Rs: According to the university's announcement, the campus game room will be shut down because it's old and relatively unused. The woman supports the university's decision, and she gives a couple of reasons for her support. She believes that video game rooms are "old-fashioned," claiming that they were popular when her parents were young. As a video game lover herself, she says that most people play games on their computers, and if many people want to play together, like in a game room, they join an online tournament. So she agrees with the university's claim that the game room should become part of the bowling alley.

CHAPTER 4

p. 81

PRACTICE 1 (*Answers will vary.*)

Main Idea: chem. defenses in plants

Details: toxins in plants = deter bugs/animals
allelopathy = chem. in soil to hurt other plants

p. 83

PRACTICE 1 (*Answers will vary.*)

Topic: Lamiaceae (mint family) plant defenses

Example 1: strong odor (from oils)

Details: taste bad to deer → don't eat
some oils repel insects (mosq. repellent)

Example 2: oils may be allelopaths

Details: henbit plant stops nearby plant growth

p. 85

PRACTICE 1 (*Answers will vary.*)

1) **From Notes → Main Idea**: chem. defenses in plants

2) **From Notes → Topic**: Lamiaceae (mint family) plant defenses
Example 1: strong odor (from oils)
Example 2: oils may be allelopaths

3) **From Notes → Details**: taste bad to deer → don't eat
some oils repel insects → (mosquito repellent)
henbit plant stops nearby plant growth

p. 87

PRACTICE 1 (*Answers will vary.*)

Rs: The passage discusses some of the ways that plants use chemicals to defend themselves. The lecture elaborates on the reading information by giving examples of the defenses used by plants in the mint family. Plants in this family often keep away animals and insects by releasing a strong odor. Plants in the mint family create this odor by releasing oils from their leaves and stems. Another chemical defense that some mint plants may use is allelopathy. The passage describes it as a process where a plant releases chemicals that affect nearby soil and discourage other plants from growing nearby. Sometimes, weeds such as henbit, a mint family member, may use allelopathy to compete successfully.

CHAPTER 5

p. 107

PRACTICE 1 (*Answers will vary.*)

Problem: woman has noisy, messy roommate
Solution 1: move to off-campus room
Solution 2: switch dorms, new roommate

p. 109

PRACTICE 1 (*Answers will vary.*)

1) **From Notes → Problem**: woman has noisy, messy roommate
2) **Preferred solution**: switch rooms, new roommate
3) **Reason 1**: woman likes convenience of on campus
   Reason 2: can request single dorm room, no roommate

p. 111

PRACTICE 1 (*Answers will vary.*)

Rs: In the conversation, the woman says that she has an inconsiderate, noisy, and messy roommate. The man recommends that the woman either look for off-campus housing or request to move to a new dorm room. Personally, I think she should move to a different on-campus dorm room. One reason staying on campus is a good idea is that the woman says she likes the convenience of being on campus. She shouldn't have to sacrifice this convenience just because she has a bad roommate. Additionally, she can probably request that the university give her a "single" dorm, which would mean that she would have a room all to herself. That way, she wouldn't have to worry about getting another bad roommate.

CHAPTER 6

p. 131

PRACTICE 1 (*Answers will vary.*)

Main Idea: bird-nesting strategies
Subtopic 1: Emperor Penguin nesting
Details: male watches egg/keeps egg on ft.
Subtopic 2: Australian malleefowl nesting
Details: makes warming mound for eggs (1 yr. process)

p. 133

PRACTICE 1 (*Answers will vary.*)

1) **From Notes → Main Idea**: bird-nesting strategies
2) **From Notes → Subtopic 1**: Emperor Penguin nesting → no nest, male keeps egg on feet and covered
   Subtopic 2: Australian malleefowl nesting → builds decomposed mound, gets warm, lays eggs (1 year)

p. 135

PRACTICE 1 (*Answers will vary.*)

Rs: The lecture discusses the nesting strategies of the Emperor Penguin and the Australian malleefowl. Emperor Penguins don't actually build a nest. Instead, the female lays an egg, and the male penguin watches over it while she leaves for months to get food. The male bird keeps the egg perched on his feet, and he covers it with his skin to keep it warm. Another odd nesting strategy is that of the malleefowl, which starts its nest by digging a hole. Next, the male bird fills the hole with materials that start to decompose and release heat. Once the nest gets hot enough, the female lays some eggs. Finally, the birds adjust the nest to keep it the right temperature until the eggs hatch. This may take almost a whole year.

CPSIA information can be obtained at www.ICGtesting.com
Printed in the USA
BVOW04s1916020915

416315BV00010B/50/P